MODERN WORLD NATIONS

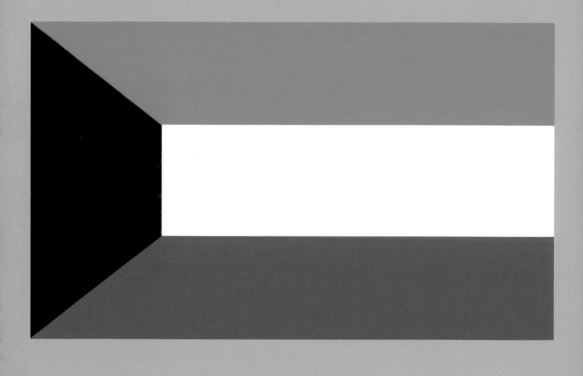

MODERN WORLD NATIONS

Kuwait

Dr. Solomon A. Isiorho
Indiana-Purdue University, Fort Wayne

Series Consulting Editor
Charles F. Gritzner
South Dakota State University

Chelsea House Publishers
Philadelphia

Frontispiece: Flag of Kuwait

Cover: Kuwait City at nightfall.

CHELSEA HOUSE PUBLISHERS

EDITOR IN CHIEF Sally Cheney
DIRECTOR OF PRODUCTION Kim Shinners
CREATIVE MANAGER Takeshi Takahashi
MANUFACTURING MANAGER Diann Grasse

Staff for KUWAIT

EDITOR Lee Marcott
PRODUCTION ASSISTANT Jaimie Winkler
PICTURE RESEARCHER 21st Century Publishing and Communications, Inc.
COVER AND SERIES DESIGNER Takeshi Takahashi
LAYOUT 21st Century Publishing and Communications, Inc.

http://www.chelseahouse.com

3 5 7 9 8 6 4 2

Library of Congress Cataloging-in-Publication Data

Isiorho, S. A. (Solomon A.)
   Kuwait / S.A. Isiorho.
     p. cm. — (Modern world nations)
Includes bibliographical references and index.
   ISBN 0-7910-7105-7 — ISBN 0-7910-6781-5 (HC)
   1. Kuwait. I. Title. II. Series.
DS247.K8 I82 2002
953.67—dc21

2002004479

Table of Contents

Kuwait

A Kuwaiti man and woman in traditional clothing walk by the coastline in Kuwait City.

Introduction to Kuwait

"War," said American writer Ambrose Bierce, "is God's way of teaching Americans geography." Although written nearly a century ago, his observation certainly holds true in regard to Kuwait. This small, little known, Middle Eastern country suddenly was thrust onto the global stage in August 1990, when it was attacked and overrun by military forces from neighboring Iraq. American and other military forces immediately intervened in defense of Kuwait in what came to be known as the "Gulf War." As a result of widespread media attention and the active participation of thousands of American troops in the conflict, Americans learned a great deal about Kuwait's geographic conditions.

Kuwait is located on the northeastern corner of the

Arabian Peninsula, bordering the northwestern edge of the Persian Gulf (known locally as the Arabian Gulf). It is located between 28 and 30 degrees north latitude, a position comparable to that of southern Texas and northernmost Mexico—both of which, like Kuwait, are also desert environments. Its shape resembles the head of a short-beaked bird, with the beak pointing westward. The country spans only about 100 miles (162 kilometers) in an east-west direction, and 125 miles (200 kilometers) north-to-south. Its 6,880 square mile (17,818 square kilometer) area is sandwiched between two much larger neighboring states.

To the south lie the parched landscapes of oil rich Saudi Arabia; to the northwest lies Iraq, also rich in oil reserves and the location of historic Mesopotamia—a fertile, low-lying plain formed by the Tigris and Euphrates Rivers that was the "Cradle of Western Civilization." Another Middle Eastern power, Iran, is located about 25 miles from the tip of northeastern Kuwait, across a small strip of Iraq that reaches the Persian Gulf. Kuwait's eastern boundary is 121 miles (195 kilometers) of coastline. In the north, the gulf is shallow and muddy, because of silt deposited by the combined Tigris and Euphrates Rivers. In the south, away from the delta, the water is deeper and much cleaner, and the coast has many fine sandy beaches.

Historically, the area that is now Kuwait was called *Qurain*. This name comes from the Arabic words *qarn* (a high hill) and *kout* (fortress). Thus, the country's name provides a strong clue to the importance of its centuries-old role as a strategic location for trade, commerce, and control of navigation in the northern Persian Gulf. Although its history can be traced back thousands of years, the modern country of Kuwait is relatively new. It began in the mid-18th century with the arrival of members of the Utub clan from what is now Saudi Arabia. This group has played an important role in Kuwait's recent history.

Kuwait's present-day importance is far greater than its size or population might suggest. With an area about the same as New Jersey and a population of just over two million (only one-quarter that of New Jersey), it might seem that the country would hardly be a "blip" on the radar screen of global importance. For two major reasons, however, Kuwait is a very important country—particularly to the United States and other Western powers. First, it has a strategic location. Kuwait lies between three much larger and more powerful countries—Saudi Arabia, Iraq, and Iran. Together, these four states possess an estimated 50 percent of Earth's known petroleum reserves. But the region is one of almost constant turbulence and—as was proved during the Gulf War—conflict can seriously disrupt the flow of vital energy resources to the United States and other countries.

Kuwait's position both on the Persian Gulf and near the spot where its neighbors almost join make its location one of the most important in the entire Middle East. A second factor of extreme importance is that Kuwait, itself, has huge energy deposits. It is a major producer of oil and natural gas and is one of the largest suppliers of petroleum to the United States.

When visiting Kuwait today, there are a surprising number of things to see and experience. The country is quite modern by Middle Eastern standards. Much of its shiny new appearance is the result of rebuilding in the aftermath of the Gulf War. Because of the country's huge oil production and relatively small population, statistically, Kuwaitis enjoy one of the world's highest per capita incomes, and gross domestic products. The country also is unique in that more than half of its population is made up

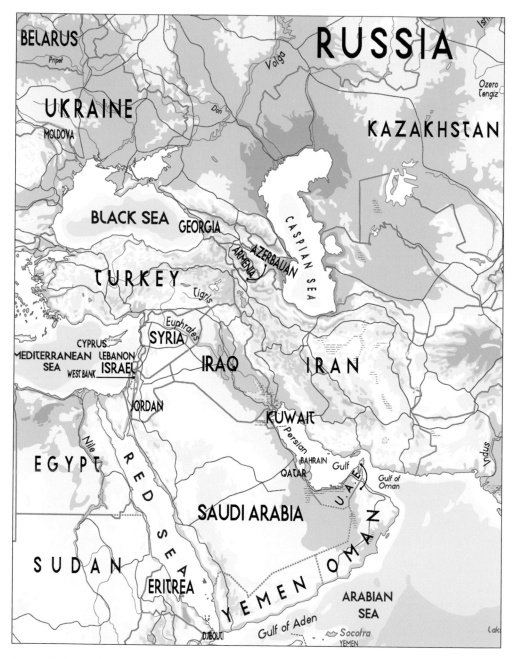

Kuwait is located on the northeastern corner of the Arabian Peninsula, bordering the northwestern edge of the Persian Gulf. It is sandwiched in between Iraq and Saudi Arabia and spans about 100 miles (162 kilometers) from east to west and about 125 miles (200 kilometers) from north to south.

of non-Kuwaitis. By some estimates, nearly three of every five people in Kuwait were born elsewhere. They flock to the country to find high paying jobs in this relatively safe and stable land.

This aerial view of a town in Kuwait shows the flat, desert land that is typical of the country.

2

The Natural Environment

K uwait's natural landscapes reflect its arid climate. Desert features—landforms, vegetation, and the lack of permanent freshwater lakes or streams—dominate the region. Much of the country is relatively flat and featureless. There are no mountains or high plateaus. In fact, the highest elevation reaches only about 1,000 feet (306 meters) above sea level. There are less than eight square miles of farmland in the entire country, and there are no surface water features to be found anywhere. Only along the coast does the environment show much change. Here, the gulf waters appear as a gigantic oasis—but the water is salty, and therefore is not suitable for drinking or irrigation without being desalinized (the removal of salt) by a costly process.

Islands

Kuwait has nine islands, of which Bubyan is the largest. It occupies an area of about 330 square miles (860 square kilometers). The island lies just off the Shatt al-Arab Delta and, in fact, was formed primarily by sediments deposited by this stream that carries the combined flow of the Tigris and Euphrates. There is very little vegetation. Small sand dunes near the shore rise above the island's otherwise flat surface. No people currently live on Bubyan. Warbah Island marks the northernmost part of Kuwait. This low island can become submerged during high tides, and like Bubyan Island it is not inhabited. Failaka, located about 12 miles (20 kilometers) east of Kuwait City, is the most scenic and famous of the country's islands. It was first settled as early as 10,000 years ago, and by 3000 B.C.E. (Before the Common Era), it was inhabited by people of the Dilmun civilization that brought both wealth and widespread recognition to the region. During the 4th century B.C.E., forces of the Greek warrior Alexander the Great built a temple on the island. The ruins are a major tourist attraction. Before the Persian Gulf War, Failaka was densely populated. Iraqis, however, devastated much of the island and planted many land mines. Today, it has no permanent population. Kuwait's other islands are small and of little importance.

The Land

The land surfaces of Kuwait were sculpted mainly by the work of wind and water. Aeolian (wind blown) features are created as winds erode sand and silt from one location and deposit these particles as sand dunes elsewhere. In the north, fluvial (river derived sediments) deposits of the ancient tributaries (branches) of the Tigris and Euphrates Rivers have created a low, flat, plains surface. Rock type and geologic history also have affected the geomorphology (landforms) of the country as different types of rock decompose at different rates.

When viewed from above, Kuwait appears as a flat land that gently dips from a high elevation of about 1,000 feet (305 meters) in the south, northeastward toward the Persian Gulf and sea level. There are no mountains or permanent rivers. The Jal az-Zor ridge provides one of the few breaks in the otherwise monotonous terrain. This 17-mile (65-kilometer) long escarpment rises abruptly like a wall northwest of Kuwait Bay. Other major landforms include the Umm Ar-Rimam depression; wadis (usually dry stream beds); several small ridges; the Mazhul and Muhayzil hills; and strange wind eroded features called "yardangs." Along the coast there are areas of cliffs, sand dunes, and coral beaches.

Coarse gravel, sand, and playa surfaces (silt and salt covered, nearly flat, surfaces of usually dry lake bottoms) make up most of Kuwait's land surface. In places where wind has removed most of the small silt or sand particles, a solid gravel surface is left behind. This stony carpet is desert pavement. As coarse sand sweeps across the desert pavement, it has the same effect as sandpaper—rocks are sanded and "polished" into a smooth surface.

Much of Kuwait is covered with sand. Winds blowing from Iran, Saudi Arabia, and other dry areas of the Middle East can transport sand and dust over hundreds of miles. Some of the sand, of course, is from local sources. In some locations, sand deposits form relatively flat surfaces; elsewhere, they form small hills, called dunes. Sand dunes are formed in different shapes and sizes. Kuwait's most common sand dune is the barchan. It is a crescent-shaped formation with its two ends, or toes, sharply pointed in the same direction the prevailing wind blows. Their spacing can be close together in a group, or as individual features scattered some distance from one another. Other dunes found in the region include elongated linear dunes, and a few parabolic dunes. Parabolic dunes are similar in shape to the barchans, except that their toes point upwind. Similar parabolic dunes are found at the Indiana Dunes

National Lakeshore along the southeastern shore of Lake Michigan. The sand dunes, along with other geomorphologic features, were greatly disturbed during the Gulf War. The fragile desert environment will take decades—and in some cases centuries—to recover.

Climate

Kuwait, like most Middle Eastern countries, has a hot, dry, desert climate, with frequent dust storms. The average annual rainfall is a scant 6 inches (15 centimeters), although the amount varies from 3 to 8 inches across the country. No place in Kuwait receives enough moisture to avoid the desert classification of its parched landscape. The country experiences four seasons, roughly corresponding to those in the United Sates and elsewhere in the Northern Hemisphere. The region's weather pattern is greatly controlled by three different air masses—huge masses of air in which the temperature, moisture content (humidity), and pressure are quite uniform. Each air mass takes on the characteristic of conditions in the source area over which it forms. The air masses that affect Kuwait's weather include a hot and humid mass that forms over the Persian Gulf (Arabian Sea); a hot and seasonally dry or humid air mass from India; and an occasional bone-chilling winter cold, dry, air mass from the interior of Asia.

In the summer, temperatures are extremely hot. In the hottest months of July and August, afternoon average high temperatures range from 108 to 115°F (46-50°C). But occasionally they may soar to a sizzling 125°F (51° C)—in the shade. The summers are accompanied by an increase in humidity that can reach 90 percent—creating some of the most miserable, steam bath like conditions on Earth. Fortunately, most buildings in Kuwait are air-conditioned. From April through the summer, strong dust storms called *tauz* shower the region with layer after layer of fine dust. Winter months bring a break from the hot, humid (though dry), and dusty summer season. In December

Swimmers enjoy cooling off in the waters surrounding Kuwait City.
Summer temperatures can reach a high of 125°F.

and January, afternoon temperatures average from 40 to 60°F
(5 to 17°C); during the night, however, they can drop to 32°F
(0°C), or lower. When the cold, dry air mass from the interior of
Asia sweeps into the region, temperatures can drop to freezing
and below for several days. Most rain falls between November
and April. As much as a third of the total annual precipitation
can fall during a single torrential storm. When this happens,
usually dry streambeds can suddenly become swollen, raging
torrents of water that sweep away anything in their path. These
flash floods, not dust storms, are the most feared natural hazard
of the desert.

Plant and Animal Life

Because of its arid conditions, all of Kuwait has a desert
ecosystem. Over 400 plant species have been identified in the
region, but most are small, widely scattered, scrub species. The

country has no woodlands, and inadequate soil moisture means that plants have to be widely scattered to survive. Desert plants are xerophytic, or drought resistant. Deep root systems, small leaves, and sharp spines are just some of the ways plants adapt to arid conditions. A rapid growth cycle is another feature that helps them to survive. When rain falls over what appears to be a totally barren desert surface, long dormant seeds suddenly spring to life. Within weeks, the once seemingly dead landscape will come alive with a spectacular display of blossoming plants. Yet only days later, all signs of life may be gone. The plants, in order for the species to survive in this harsh desert environment, have gone through their entire life cycle in a matter of a few weeks during which life-giving moisture was available for growth.

Animal life is scant. Few species are adapted to the country's harsh environment. Additionally, many species that were able to survive in this arid habitat were destroyed by the ravages of the Gulf War. It is too early to tell what long-term effects the war's environmental changes will have on the region's flora and fauna. Small, often nocturnal, life-forms abound. They include a variety of insects, including spiders, scorpions, crickets, locusts, and cockroaches. There are also a number of snakes (including more than 20 poisonous varieties) and lizards. Small animals include various rodents, hares, and rabbits. More than 300 bird species have been identified in Kuwait, most of which are migratory, hence, seasonal.

Water

The Persian Gulf, and its extension, Kuwait Bay, are the most prominent water features in Kuwait. The bay provides natural protection for the port of Kuwait City. For thousands of years, the Gulf has provided Kuwaitis with a reliable source of fish and pearls. It has also given them a navigational pathway for travel, trade, and commerce. Today, the gulf water has taken on a new importance—through the

Water from the Persian Gulf must be processed in desalinization plants, such as the one shown here, before the people of Kuwait can use it.

process of seawater desalinization, it is the source of most of the country's domestic and agricultural water supply.

Other than the gulf, Kuwait has no permanent water bodies. Streams and basins can rapidly fill with water after an infrequent torrential downpour, but they soon become dry once again. A map of Kuwait's cities also shows the locations where—at least at one time—fresh water was available. Populations have long clustered around oasis sites where springs or wells provide life-giving supplies of water in an otherwise parched desert landscape.

"Oasis" is the name given to any place in a desert region where fresh water is available by any means. Such sites are often along rivers, around lakes, or near springs or wells. All of

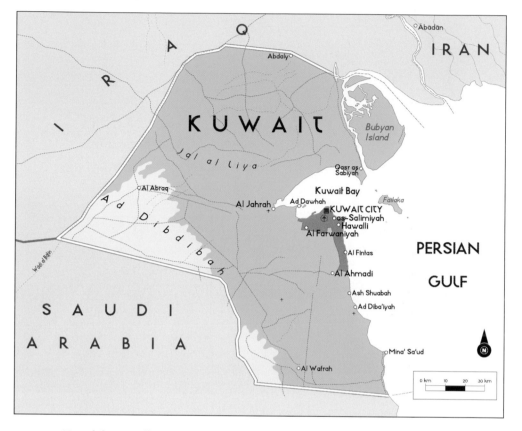

Kuwait is a small country about the size of New Jersey and has an estimated population of just over 2 million people. It is an arid land with beautiful coastlines along the Persian Gulf. Rather than being spread out across the country most people live in a city and most cities are not far from the coast.

Kuwait's oases were built up around springs or wells, since the country has no permanent rivers or lakes. In areas of sand dunes, the sands may create depressions that for a short time collect and hold some rainwater. Usually dry lakebeds also hold water after it rains, although they are covered with a layer of salt that rapidly makes the water useless. Water trapping sand and and lakebed depressions are found throughout much of the country. For centuries, they have been important watering holes for Bedouins (a nomadic desert tribe) and their camels. Although in the past there were a number of oases in

Kuwait, today only one true oasis remains. It is an area called Sebihiya, located south of the country's capital, Kuwait City.

Natural Regions

Kuwait is divided into four natural regions, the Northern, Western, Southern, and Coastal Provinces. The Northern Province, as is true of others, shows evidence that the area was once much wetter. Thousands of years ago, during the Ice Age, many of today's desert areas received much more precipitation than they do today. Streams flowing across the region formed large channels, and many basins filled with water to become lakes. Now, with a much drier climate, the wadis (dry streambeds) are almost always dry and the playas (dry lakebeds) are rarely filled. The Northern Province also has many sand dunes and long, linear ridges. Very few people live in this region.

The Western Province is largely a barren desert wilderness covered mainly by desert pavement, or gravel. Major features of the region include a large valley, Wadi al-Batin, that forms the boundary between Iraq and Kuwait; a large alluvial fan created by the delta of ancient rivers that flowed from Saudi Arabia; the large Umm ar-Rimam depressions, some of which have playa lakes; and dune fields covering around 154 square miles (400 square kilometers). The Southern Province covers the southern lowland part of Kuwait. Its surface is sandy and rocky in most places. The Coastal Province includes Kuwait Bay, where there are many beach sediments and wetlands. Coastal sand dunes, marshes, cliffs, and ridges can also be seen in this province.

It might appear that nature has treated Kuwait very unkindly. However, the country is blessed (although some might believe cursed!) with one very rich and abundant resource—"black gold," or petroleum. Its importance is discussed in several later chapters.

This ancient relief from the Palace of Sargon in Mesopotamia illustrates the transport of wood by boat in the eighth century B.C.E.

3

A Proud Past

K uwait has a proud past. The small country likes to think of itself as the "Pride of the Persian Gulf." People have lived in the region for at least 8,000 years. Most of what we know about early Kuwait has come from archaeologists (scientists who study of the remains of past human activities such as culture, monuments, and relics), and early written records. The country's geographical location, including the position of its capital and chief port, Kuwait City, makes it a strategically important area in the Persian Gulf. Historically, Kuwait took advantage of its strategic position between fertile and highly productive agricultural areas that were homes to large and powerful civilizations—the Nile Valley to the west, Mesopotamia to the northwest, Persia to the northeast, and the Indus valley and India to the east. This gave Kuwaitis an advantage in developing regional trade and commerce.

Early Ties to Mesopotamia

In ancient times, perhaps 5,000 to 7,000 years ago, Mesopotamia—the fertile land lying northwest of Kuwait between the Tigris and Euphrates Rivers—became perhaps the world's first and most important early area of food production. In this parched desert land, the rivers provided water for irrigation, livestock, and human settlement. During flood stages, streams also deposited the rich sediments that became the soils on which crops thrived. These early farming peoples became the "roots" of Western civilization and culture.

With a productive agriculture that provided a surplus of food, not all people had to farm. Some could move into a new kind of settlement—villages. Life was much different in towns, and people had to develop new skills and trades. They began to specialize in a variety of crafts, businesses, and services. With the establishment of communities and new trades came different job opportunities, such as merchants, traders, soldiers, and administrators. At this time religion, too, began to become formalized. And there was a need to keep detailed records; hence, Mesopotamians were among the first people to develop advanced forms of writing and mathematics. With a growing supply of food and an ever-increasing diversity of trades, people were able to develop even larger communities, or cities.

Cities need many different things to survive and grow. Yet Mesopotamia lacked many essentials, including wood for building and minerals for its industries. People of the region turned to trading for these needed items, or to importing them from other lands. Also, with a surplus of food and other items, they soon realized that trade with other lands and peoples could bring a handsome profit. Ultimately, Kuwait—with its long coastline, excellent harbor, and strategic location on the Persian Gulf—was able to profit by playing a major role in the trade that took place between Mesopotamia and India, and elsewhere in the region.

Although early life along the coast was not always easy, it was often more difficult for the Bedouin. These nomadic peoples' lives revolved around their herds of camels, sheep, and goats. Much of their time was spent wandering from oasis to oasis in search of water, grazing land, and food for themselves and their animals. They often spent hotter summer months near towns or other oasis sites, where water and shade were available. In the cooler, wetter, winter months they would lead their herds into the desert.

Ancient Kuwait

The land known today as Kuwait was first occupied in about 8000 B.C.E., by Mesolithic (Middle Stone Age) people. They left but scant evidence of their presence. Between 2200 and 1800 B.C.E., people of the Bronze Age Dilmun civilization settled Failaka Island. This wealthy and powerful trading empire thrived because of its strategic position. The western Persian Gulf was located along important trade routes that linked the Indus Valley in present-day Pakistan and India, with Mesopotamia. In about 600 B.C.E., a group of people called the Heelless settled on Failaka Island. Because of this strategic location, they, too, became a major link in the trade between rich lands to both the northwest and east. Kuwait has taken advantage of this strategic geographic position throughout most of its history.

In 325 B.C.E., the Greek warrior Alexander the Great sent a fleet of ships from India into the Persian Gulf. Some of his soldiers settled on Failaka Island. This site was chosen because of its close proximity to the southern gateway to Mesopotamia and its wealth—the delta region of the combined Tigris and Euphrates Rivers. They remained in Kuwait for less than a century, however. Today, evidence of their presence more than 2,000 years ago is found in ruins of their settlements, including

Failaka Island was a strategic link in ancient trade routes. An aerial view shows the ruins of a settlement from thousands of years ago.

carvings of Greek gods they left behind. In about 250 B.C.E., the entire Persian Gulf region fell under control of a powerful Persian dynasty, the Parthians. Several centuries later, they were followed by the Sassanians. This powerful dynasty, also from Persia, held control over the area for four centuries, until its military defeat by Muslim Arabs in 632 A.D. The region was highly prized because of its importance to trade. This is the primary reason it had changed hands so many times over the centuries. In the trade between east and west, Greeks and later the Romans favored a route through the Red Sea and into the Indian Ocean. Persians, on the other hand, favored the Persian Gulf route for trade, because of its close proximity to Mesopotamia. During the seventh century, however, those empires that had been involved in east-west trade fell into decline. So, too, did Kuwait's fortunes—dependent primarily on this trade—rapidly fade. For a thousand years, it became part of a remote, nameless, unimportant, and forgotten region of the world.

Early Settlers of Modern Kuwait

The history of modern Kuwait is traced to 1710, when it was settled by Bani Utub groups. The Utub clan belongs to a group of families of the Anaiza tribe. This group, led by the Sabah family, was a part of the Anaiza tribe from modern-day Saudi Arabia. The Utub probably came to Kuwait to escape a terrible drought. In the 1750s, the Anaiza tribe's Sabah family began its dynasty in ruling over the land of Kuwait. The ruler, or sheik, was to govern over the land of Kuwait and to represent the country's people in foreign matters, most notably those involving the Ottoman Empire.

During the reign of the first Sabah, Kuwait became part of the huge and powerful Ottoman (Turkish) Empire that spread from Constantinople (today's Istanbul) to span much of south-western Asia, including the Arabian Peninsula. Under Ottoman control, Kuwait was a province of Turkey, although the Turks did not physically rule the country. When the Ottoman did act to gain more control over Kuwait, Sheik Mubarak I (who was then ruler) acted tactfully to retain its independence. He aligned the country with some powerful allies in the region, notably, the British. A treaty was signed between Kuwait and Britain in 1899. It defined Kuwait as being an independent country under British protection. Britain would protect the small, weak country from foreign attack and also provide support for the sheik's upkeep. In return, Sheik Mubarak agreed to certain conditions. He could not make treaties with other countries, he would not allow agents from other countries to enter Kuwait, and he would not give up any of the country's territory. Following the outbreak of World War I in 1914, Kuwait formally became a British protectorate.

After the rule of Sheik Mubarak, his sons, Sheik Jaber (1915-1917) and Sheik Salim (1917-1921), took control of the government. From this time forward, all rulers of Kuwait have been descendants of the two brothers.

Sheik Ahmad al-Jaber al-Sabah ruled from 1921 until his death in 1950. He was followed by Sheik Abdullah al-Salim al-Sabah from 1950 to 1965. By 1961, the British had withdrawn much of their influence, including their special court system. Kuwait began to exercise its own legal jurisdiction and to take control of other aspects of governing. On June 19, 1961, Kuwait finally gained complete independence from Britain.

Border Disputes

Many countries around the world have experienced border disputes with their neighbors. Kuwait is no exception. Its invasion by military forces from neighboring Iraq in August 1990 involved such a dispute. This segment of Kuwait's history is discussed in chapter 8.

Historically, Kuwait and Iraq (as well as many other lands in the Middle East) were provinces of the Ottoman Empire. The ruler of the two provinces was sometimes based in Iraq. The boundary between the two present-day countries has long been contested by Iraq, which claims that Kuwait is part of its territory. This was why Iraq tried to annex Kuwait in 1990. The border between Iraq and Kuwait was determined in 1913 by Turkey, which then was in control of the two countries. The border between Kuwait and Saudi Arabia was established in 1922. Iraq accepted the boundary in 1923 when it obtained its independence from Turkey. In 1963, however, Iraq changed the boundary to its advantage. A neutral zone of 2,000 square miles (5,180 square kilometers) was established during this time. The neutral zone was divided in 1969, and in July 2000 the maritime boundary dividing the sea between the two countries was ratified. Iraq, nonetheless, invaded Kuwait one month later.

Kuwait's prime minister Crown Prince Saad al-Abdullah al-Salim al-Sabah (left) is the current member of the Sabah dynasty to lead the government.

Because of the continuing dispute over the location of Kuwait's boundary with Iraq, it is not possible to give precise figures for the country's total area.

Kuwait's Rulers

For more than 250 years, all rulers of Kuwait have been from a single family, the Al-Sabah. Most ruling families in the region came to power by force. This was not the case, however, with what was to become the Sabah dynasty. This powerful family arrived in Kuwait in 1716. By 1752, it was chosen by the Kuwaiti people to lead them. The family had to administer the Kuwaiti community and to carry on relations with neighboring sheiks to ensure the safety of the townspeople.

Unlike the modern day sheiks, early rulers were often very poor. An 1841 eyewitness account by a British resident in the gulf reads, "Both himself (Jabir I) and his Sons are perhaps among the worst dressed and most ill-lodged residents in the place. Excepting a small duty levied upon the sales and purchases of the Bedouins who resort to his Town, the Shaikh collects no taxes or customs." Faced with continuous threats from the Ottoman Empire, Egypt, and other powers of the time, the Al-Sabah became skillful in negotiating with every regional leader to protect their independence and to encourage trade and commerce. The sheiks were not paid. They depended on the merchants' benevolence for their daily living. Since 1752, the Sabah family has ruled Kuwait, and as such, their rule has been called the Sabah dynasty.

The Al-Sabah Dynasty

Kuwait City was established around 1672, and the Sabah family arrived in Kuwait City in 1716. About 36 years later, the first sheik from the Sabah family, Sabin bin Jaber al-Sabah was named Kuwait's first ruler. No one really knew much about his beginning other than he came with the rest of the Utub clan and that his father's name was Jaber. Traditional accounts say there were three Utub families: Alkhalifa, Al-Jalahima, and Al-Sabah, and each was assigned different responsibilities. Alkhalifa, who were wealthy, took charge of Kuwait's lucrative pearling industry and trade; the Al-Jalahima commanded the boats; and Al-Sabah, provided political leadership, giving and maintaining law and order and handling Kuwait's foreign relations.

Sabah and his sons enjoyed the cooperation of local merchants and Bedouin (nomadic tribesmen) leaders. This made it possible for Kuwait to become a major trading center. Ships carrying valuable trade items from Persia and India, as well as from other areas within the Persian Gulf, brought their valuable cargo to Kuwait's protected harbor.

And the hardy Bedouin tribesmen provided the Sabah with protection and power. Sheik Sabah bin Jaber ruled from 1756 to 1762.

Sabah I was followed by his youngest son, Abdullah. During Sheik Abdullah's reign, many important changes came to Kuwait. Bigger and stronger ships were built, and Kuwait became a major boat-building center in the Persian Gulf. The country and its people became widely known and respected for reliability and integrity during his reign. While he was in power, a militant Bedouin religious group called the Wahhabis (also known as Ikhwan) tried to spread their own version of Islam. This resulted in the attack of Kuwait's traditional overlords, the Bani Khalid. Abdullah lost one of his sons during one of these skirmishes. Under Abdullah's able leadership, Kuwait's independence was maintained. And both Abdullah's virtues and the fine spirit of the Kuwaitis became known throughout the region. Kuwait was looked upon so favorably by many of its neighbors that large numbers of Iraqis and Persians moved to the country. Sheik Abdullah I had a long and very successful rule, from 1762 to 1812.

Sheik Abdullah's son, Jaber I bin Abdullah I bin Sabah I, was the next in line. But he had a disagreement with his father and left Kuwait, moving to the nearby island country of Bahrain. In Jaber's absence, his cousin Muhammad Salma Sabah assumed power. Kuwaitis preferred Jaber I, however, and urged him to return home from Bahrain. On his return, he carried on his father's legacy. Friendly relationships were maintained with the British. During his reign, there were several military conflicts in the region. Jaber I was very diplomatic in his relations with other nations. He was successful in keeping Kuwait out of the wars, a factor that contributed greatly to helping make the country even more prosperous. Jaber I helped the Ottoman Turks, and he was richly rewarded. He became the first member of the Sabah family to gain enough wealth to become at least partially independent of the powerful merchants. Because of his wealth, he was able to generously feed the poor. For this help, his subjects gave him the title of Jaber al-Aish (meaning, Jaber of Rice). Sheik Jaber I also had a very long reign, which lasted from 1812 to 1859.

Sheik Sabah II ascended the throne at the age of 80 after the death of his father, Sheik Jaber I. Sheik Sabah II helped his father govern during his reign. He represented his father during negotiations of a maritime treaty with the British. He also maintained the traditional neutrality in Kuwait's foreign affairs. Like his father, through diplomacy he was able to keep from being entangled in the region's conflicts. During his 1859-1866 reign, he also continued his father's policy of helping feed the poor.

The next ruler was Sheik Abdullah II, who was best known for aligning Kuwait with the Ottomans. He was given the title Qaimmaqam (meaning provincial subgovernor). Abdullah II aided the Turkish regional ruler by offering Kuwait as a port for his naval fleet. This wise move no doubt saved Kuwait from an Ottoman military invasion. During his 1866-1892 reign, Kuwaiti merchants continued to prosper.

At the death of Sheik Abdullah II, his second son, Muhammad I, took control of Kuwait from 1892 to 1896. He was in charge of administration and foreign affairs; one of his brothers was placed in charge of financial affairs, and another brother controlled the military. Sheik Abdullah II was greatly influenced by a pro-Ottoman Iraq. Many Kuwaitis, however, feared that their country might lose its independence if they became too closely tied to their larger and more powerful northern neighbor. In fear that they might become a part of Ottoman controlled Iraq, the Kuwaitis turned to Muhammad's brother, Mubarak, for help. Because of the widespread support he received from the public, Mubarak felt strong enough to take over country's leadership.

Sheik Mubarak I came into power in 1896 by killing his two brothers (Muhammad I and Jarrah). This was the first time a sheik rose to power by force in this normally peaceful and law-abiding country. Some Kuwaitis think of him as having been a tyrant, whereas others see him as having been a savior. Mubarak was a resourceful ruler. He was Qaimmaqam of Kuwait, a British protected person and an independent ruler. His most important achievement in the eyes of many Kuwaitis was keeping Kuwait from the grasp of Ottoman control. Also, the British declared Kuwait an independent sheikdom under British protection during his rule. Mubarak I died in 1915 after contracting malaria, thus ending his reign.

After the passing of Mubarak I, his son Sheik Jaber II took control of the government. His rule was short, from 1915 until his death in 1917. With World War I raging in Europe, Jaber II took a very strong pro-British stance in order to ensure his country's protection by British forces.

Sheik Salim came to power after the death of Jaber II. He made some changes in the administration of Kuwait City by dividing the town into wards with each having a ruler, or *mkhtar* (mayor). He campaigned against immorality and urged Kuwaitis to go back to their more traditional religious practices. His reign lasted from 1917 to 1921.

The next ruler was Sheik Ahmad. Kuwaitis wanted him to rule with the consultation of a council that represented their interests and to abide by the various treaties signed with the British by former rulers. Ahmad led the country from 1921 until 1950.

After Sheik Ahmad's death, Sheik Abdullah III al-Salim came on the throne. Kuwaitis almost unanimously rank Abdullah III as the greatest of the country's modern rulers. It was during his reign that the British gave up control over many of Kuwait's domestic matters, including currency and the postal service. He also called in Egyptian lawyers to give the

During the rule of Sheik Abdullah III al-Salim, Kuwait gained independence from Great Britain. Abdullah III ruled from 1950 until his death in 1965.

country a judicial and legislative system. During his reign, Kuwait gained its independence from Great Britain. The new country got its own currency and joined world bodies like the United Nations (UN), the Organization of Petroleum Exporting Countries (OPEC), and the Arab League. He died in 1965, after having reigned for 15 years.

Following the death of Sheik Abdullah III, Sheik Sabah III ascended to the throne. He had held several key positions, including head of public security, director of foreign affairs, deputy prime minister, and later prime minister. Sabah III was regarded as a special friend of the people during his 1965 to 1977 reign.

Sheik Jaber III, who became the next ruler of Kuwait, was born in 1926. Like his immediate predecessor, he had held several key positions including that of prime minister before becoming the country's leader. His reign began in 1977 and continues as this book is published. Waiting in line to succeed Jaber as Kuwait's next ruler is the Crown Prince His Highness Sheik Saad al-Abdullah al-Salim IV.

Muslims follow the Islamic religion as it is set forth in the Qur'an (Koran). This boy is reciting verses from the Qur'an for his teacher.

4

Islam in Kuwait

I slam is the official state religion of Kuwait. An estimated 90 percent of the country's people are Muslims, the name given those who follow the faith. The word "Islam" means total submission to the will of God. For many of the world's people, religion is an important force in their lives. It can play a significant role in influencing culture. This chapter explains Islam, Muslim beliefs and practices, and the many ways the religion has affected Kuwaiti culture. One example is the country's laws, most of which are based on Islamic law, known as *Sharia*. Kuwait has a small number of Christians, amounting to about 6 percent of the population. Followers of other religions, or nonreligious people, make up the remaining few percent.

Islam

Many Americans first learned about Islam after the tragic events of September 11, 2001. Political terrorists, who happened to be Muslims, were responsible for the destruction of the World Trade Center towers in New York City and the partial destruction of the Pentagon building in Washington, D.C. Many others perhaps became aware of Islam from television programs showing rock-throwing Palestinians, or other scenes triggered by the long-standing conflict between Palestinians and Israelis. With such negative publicity, it may be difficult for many Americans to realize that the vast majority of people who follow the Islamic religion are kind, hardworking, and peace loving. The Holy Book of Islam, the Qur'an (Koran in English), does not teach destruction of innocent lives and properties. It, like the Bible, does not condone killing. All religions, including Christianity, have had their terrorists. Such individuals often use religion as a "mask" to cover their real intentions.

Nearly all Kuwaiti Arabs are Muslims who follow the teachings of the Muslim holy book, the Qur'an (meaning "the recitation"). The Qur'an, like the Bible, forbids stealing, lying, adultery, and murder. It teaches its followers to honor their parents, show kindness, protect orphans and widows, and give money to the poor. Many Muslims believe that life on Earth is a period of testing and preparation for the life to come. They also believe that people will be accountable for their actions after death, and will be judged based on their works and deeds, as well as their knowledge of the Qur'an. Because of the latter incentive, many devout Muslims learn to recite the Qur'an from memory.

The Five Basic Pillars of Islam

Islamic belief is built around five basic "pillars." Each pillar can be thought of as a "guidepost" for proper living along life's pathway. These rules by which many Muslims live are as follow:

Pillar 1. The *Shahada* (profession of faith). This states that there is only one God and he is Allah and that the prophet Muhammad was God's messenger. Allah is the Arabic word for God.

Pillar 2. *Salat* (prayers). A Muslim should pray at five specific times each day. Times are determined mainly by the sun's position. The first prayer is just before sunrise, and the second at noon, the third when the sun is between noon and sunset position, the fourth is after sunset, and the fifth is after dark. These prayers are said facing the direction of Mecca; hence, when praying in North America, Muslims will face the east.

Pillar 3. *Zakat* (almsgiving). Islam demands that alms (money) be given to the poor. This practice is different than tithing, or contributions made to a church based on one's income.

Pillar 4. *Saum* (fasting). This rule involves avoiding food and drink from dawn to dusk during the ninth month of the lunar calendar. The period of fast is known as Ramadan. Any Muslim who is physically able is expected to participate (usually from age 10 to 12 and above).

Pillar 5. *Hajj* (pilgrimage). Every Muslim is encouraged to travel to Mecca at least once in their lifetime if they are physically and financially able to travel. When the religious obligation has been fulfilled, the individual gains the title Alhaji (for men), or Alhaja (for women). The person then can be addressed by the title, just as someone with a Ph.D. degree is called "doctor."

There are other lesser pillars that all Muslims share. They include the *jihad*, or struggles for the triumph of God's word on Earth—the requirement to do good works, and to avoid evil thoughts, words, and deeds. The term jihad is often incorrectly translated in the Christian world to mean holy war. It actually means "effort" in Arabic. For example, preaching is a form of a jihad.

The Muslims' articles of faith can be summarized as follows: Belief in Allah or one God; belief in the prophets and the messengers of Allah; belief in the books of Revelation sent by Allah; belief in the angels of Allah; belief in the final day of judgment; and belief in Allah's foreknowledge. The Muslims' articles of faith are similar to those of Christians or Jews in some regards. Both Christians and Jews believe in one God, the Torah or Old Testament, and the Psalms. The Muslims believe in the prophets in the Jewish Torah and the Christian Bible. However, many Muslims hold different views than those of the Jews and Christians. Muslims, for example, think of Jesus Christ as having been one of the prophets, and that Muhammad was the last true prophet. We will look at more examples of the similarities between the Qur'an, Bible, and Torah after examining a brief history of Islam.

Prophet Muhammad al-Mustafa

To understand Islam, it is necessary to know something about the beginning and the founder of the religion. Muhammad al-Mustafa, born in Mecca, Saudi Arabia, in 572 A.D., founded Islam. He was born two months after his father died. Muhammad was raised by his uncle, Abu Talib, who was a trader. Although he belonged to the important Koreish Arabian tribe, he was poor. He did have some camels, goats, and a slave girl (a practice that was common at that time, both in Arabia and many other places in the world, including much of Europe). Muhammad became a skilled horse rider. His knowledge of animals earned him a job working for a wealthy woman, tending her herd of camels. Later, in 595, he married the rich and much older widower named Khadija.

Muslims are encouraged to make a pilgrimage to the holy city of Mecca, the place of Muhammad's birth and triumph in battle to claim the city for Islam.

Muhammad was aware of Judaism and Christianity. But he was deeply concerned because some Christians and Jews of the time worshiped idols. He decided to go to Mount Hira, a peak located north of Mecca, to pray and meditate. Muhammad could afford to go to the mountain each year. Having married a rich woman, he no longer had to work to be able to survive. During one of his visits to the mountain, he claimed to have received a vision from God. He shared this experience with his wife, who urged him to continue his quest for Allah (God) and to share his vision with others. Muslims believe that Muhammad received most revelations directly from God, and others from the angel Gabriel.

Muhammad declared himself a chosen prophet of God and started preaching his message in Mecca. He gained some followers from his teaching. In 622, some of these followers told Muhammad of a plot by some of his enemies to kill him. Fearful for his life, he fled from the coastal city of Mecca and traveled northward some 250 miles (400 kilometers) to the inland city of Medina. This journey marks the beginning of the Islamic calendar. This year is called 1 A.H. ("after Hegira," meaning flight, or migration). In 630, he returned to Mecca, leading his followers in a successful battle to claim the city and with it Arabia for his faith. The prophet Muhammad was both devoutly religious and a strong and able leader.

Muhammad died in 632, two years after his return to Mecca. His sayings and visions were collected into a book, known as the Qur'an. The book has 114 chapters and 6,236 verses. While Muhammad was alive, the Bedouins accepted his teachings and made a pledge of allegiance to him as the Prophet of Islam. The Bedouins were largely nomadic, and through their travel and trading they successfully spread Islam to the rest of the Arabian Peninsula, including Kuwait. When the prophet died, there was some dissention revolving around the possible selection of a successor. Muslims, however, believe there could be no other prophet. Muhammad, they believed, was the "Seal of the Prophets," that is, the final prophet.

Islamic Sects

Today, there are two major Muslim sects: the Sunnis and Shiites. About 85 percent of the world's Muslims belong to the Sunni sect. The Shiites, however, tend to be much more fundamental in their interpretation of the Qur'an. Sunni Muslims are the majority in Kuwait.

After the death of the prophet Muhammad, Abu Bakr became the elected leader of Islam. Bakr was one of the earliest converts to Islam; he was also a trusted friend and father-in-law to his predecessor. He took the title Khakifa Rasul Allah (successor to the messenger of God). The khakifa (caliph) is an elected position that includes heading the religious group and serving as the political leader of a community. Before he died,

Caliph Abu Bakr selected Umar as his successor. At this time there was considerable disagreement about the selection of Bakr as caliph. The division of Islam into the Sunni and Shiite sects is a result of these disagreements.

A group of Muslims that believed in following the established customs of selecting a successor became known as the Sunnis. Another group disagreed with the selection of any successor. They believed that Muhammad had named Ali b. Abi Talib (Ali Ibin Abe Taleb), his cousin and son-in-law (married to the prophet's daughter Fatima), as his successor. The followers of Ali became known as Shi'at 'Ali (the party of Ali), or Shi'a (Shi'at, or Shiite) Muslims. According to the doctrine of this group, only Ali and his direct descendants can be the original source of religious instruction and guidance. They believed that the teachings of the Qur'an cannot be understood through human reasoning, requiring an imam (spiritual guide and leader) to explain its meaning. Shiites believe that imams are inerrant (cannot make mistakes) in interpreting the law and tradition of Islam. The Shiites, in turn, split into two other groups, forming the "Twelvers" (Fatimas) and "Seveners" (Ismailis). The names are based on the number of imams. After the twelfth imam disappeared mysteriously in 878, Shiite religious scholars assumed his office. They still await the return of the "rightly guided one," as the last imam was known. Ayatollahs (signs of God) are the joint caretakers of the imam's office until he returns at the end of time.

Similarities Between Muslims, Christians, and Jews

Despite the many divergent views of Kuwait's various religions, Muslims, Christians, and Jews have certain things in common—including monotheism, the belief in one God. The first commandment of the three religions deals with submission to God: "Hear, O Israel! The Lord our God is one Lord (God)! Therefore you shall adore the Lord your God with all your heart, with all your soul, with all your mind, and with all your strength." (Deuteronomy 6:4-5; Qur'an 3:18). This acknowledges God's absolute authority.

Each of the three faiths has a holy book: the Qur'an for Muslims, the Bible for Christians, and the Torah for Jews. There are some similarities between the Qur'an and the Christian Bible. For example, the Qur'an (2:256) states, "Let there be no compulsion in religion; truth stands out clear from error," while the similar biblical (John 8:32) passage reads "And you shall know the truth; and the truth shall set you free." Muslims, Jews, and Christians believe in Abraham as the father of nations. The sayings of the prophet Muhammad mention the prophets of the Torah and Bible as seen in this quotation, "O you who believe, believe in God and His Apostle and the book which He has sent down to His Apostle, and the scripture which He has sent down formerly. Whosoever denies God and His angels and His Books and His Apostles and the last day has strayed from the truth" (Surah 4:135). The three religions believe in one God as the creator of the world, and that he is omnipotent (all authority), omniscient (complete knowledge), a judge, and merciful.

There are, however, striking differences between the three religions. Muslims believe that their religion is an evolving one, as humankind has been guided by a series of prophets, starting from Abraham and ending with Muhammad. Muslims believe that children are born without sin, contrarily to what Christians believe. Muslims also believe that Jesus was a prophet and nothing more than that. They also do not believe that Jesus was crucified, as is indicated in this quotation: "They claimed that they killed the Messiah, Jesus, the son of Mary, the messenger of God! In fact, they never killed him; they never crucified him; they were led to believe that they did." (Qur'an 4:157)

The Hadith (Sunna), a record of sayings and deeds of Muhammad and early Muslims, is read along with the Qur'an

The Qur'an sets forth the guidelines for the Islamic religion.

by Muslims. This book contains historical and biographical information on early Islam and Muslims. The Qur'an and Hadith together form a comprehensive guide to the spiritual, ethical, and social life of the Sunni Muslims. Some Muslims rely solely on the Qur'an alone and do not consider the Hadith a holy book.

Mosques

The Muslim place of worship is the mosque. Several mosque designs exist, but they all have at least one minaret (tower from which a caller announces the time for prayer) and are open for people to place mats on the floor for prayers. Kuwait has several mosques, the largest and most famous being the Grande Mosque in Kuwait City. All Muslims are required to observe *salat*, the obligatory ritual of praying five times each day at prescribed times. During those times, there are rituals

The largest mosque in Kuwait is the Grande Mosque in Kuwait City.

and purifications that have to be done before the prayers. Believers of Islam wash their faces, arms to elbow, wipe their heads with wet hands, and wash their feet to the ankle in observance of Islamic rules. Genuflections (bending of the knees) similar to those performed by Roman Catholics and prostrations are some of the marks of a praying Muslim.

The Call to Prayer (*Azaan*)

Muslims gather together to pray on Fridays (usually around noon). This congregational prayer on Fridays is called *Salat-ul-Jum'a*. The call to prayer (*Azaan*) is usually made through loudspeakers with the saying of the words "*Allah u*

Akbar" (God is great) four times and ending it with "*Laa Elaaha Ella Allah*" (There is no god besides God). On Fridays, men go to the Mosques to pray and hear a sermon from an imam (Muslim religious leader). Women usually pray at home, but can pray in mosques if they are separated from the men. At the end of Friday prayers, there is an exchange of greetings or congratulations offered to one another. Perhaps the most commonly spoken phrase is a form of greeting between Arabs, hence Muslims, *Assalam alaikum* (peace be unto you).

Christianity

For an Islamic state, Kuwaitis are quite tolerant of other religions, including Christianity. Christians are allowed complete freedom to worship and be involved in other church-related activities. The state recognizes three principal churches: The National Evangelical Church of Kuwait, the Roman Catholic Church, and the Roman Orthodox Church. Religions with smaller numbers of followers align themselves with one of these principal churches. Most of the Christians are foreign workers, although there are about 200 native Kuwaiti Christian families.

In 2001 Kuwaiti men performed during a celebration marking the 10th anniversary of Kuwait's liberation from Iraqi occupation.

5

The People and Culture of Kuwait

Population

K uwait, a small country about the size of New Jersey, has an estimated population of just over 2 million, compared to New Jersey's 8.4 million people. Kuwait's population density is about 300 per square mile (115 per square kilometer), but this figure is misleading. Rather than being equally spread out across the country, nearly everyone lives in cities. In fact, the country is unique in that it is one of the few with 100 percent of its population classified as being urban. More than half of all Kuwaitis live in communities bordering the Persian Gulf. The largest cities (with 2002 population estimates) are as-Salimiyah (150,000), Jalib ash-Shuyuh (115,000), Hawalli (85,000), and Khitan-al-Janubiya (85,000). The capital, Kuwait City, has a population of approximately 32,000.

Oil was discovered in Kuwait in the early 20th century. The many new oil-related jobs served as a magnet that attracted a steady stream of people from other lands. So many foreigners came to Kuwait that today Kuwaitis are a minority population in their own country. In 1990, before the Gulf War, Kuwaitis represented only 27 percent of their country's population. In an attempt to reverse this trend, the government began to restrict the influx of people into the country. It would like to see Kuwaitis make up at least 50 percent of the nation's people. The government also is encouraging Kuwaitis to have more children by giving them a financial incentive for every child a couple has. Today, the average family size in Kuwait is just over eight members, although today women, on average, give birth to only about three children.

The government's efforts to increase the native population ratio may be working. By 1994, the Kuwaiti population had risen to 37 percent of the total, and by 2000 it had increased to 45 percent of the nation's population.

Any country's population can be seen visually in what demographers (scientists who study statistics of the human population) call a population pyramid. Pyramids show populations by age and gender. They can also give a picture of future population trends.

An examination of the population distribution shows that it is growing slowly. The young population, under 15 years of age, is smaller than the group in their childbearing years (15 to 44 years). This suggests that Kuwait's population will decrease in time unless immigration from other countries is increased. This is not likely, however, since the government continues its attempt to increase the percentage of Kuwaitis living in the country.

Kuwait's population has increased from its sharp decline in the early 1990s as a result of the war. During the past decade, it has risen from a low of about 1.5 million to a 2002 estimate of perhaps 2.2 to 2.3 million. A local Arabic daily paper, *Al-rai Al-Aam,* quoting the Ministry of Planning, reported the 2001 population at 2,693,000, a figure much higher than most estimates. Taking a regular census is costly and difficult. Many countries, unable to undertake a regular count of their population, simply guess at the numbers.

Life expectancy in Kuwait is one of the longest in the Middle East. The average Kuwaiti can expect to live 77 years. Most of the Kuwaiti population is young, with about 60 percent being under 30 years old. With an aging population, it appears that Kuwait will have to continue depending on a largely foreign workforce to fill its jobs.

Early Kuwaiti Peoples and Culture

Today, nearly all of Kuwait's people live in a modern urban setting. But most "native" people can trace their ancestry to traditional tribal societies living in Saudi Arabia, or elsewhere in the region. Many are descendants of the Utub group, or other early tribal settlers who came to the gulf shores from the interior of the Arabian Peninsula. Others came from Iraq or Persia (Iran). Upon arriving in Kuwait, many of these people of desert stock gave up their traditional activities. Rather than following herds of livestock from oasis to oasis, they settled on the Persian Gulf coast. Here, they adapted themselves to a life revolving around the sea—trading, fishing, pearl diving, or boat building.

Most Kuwaitis are Arab in origin, however, and the country maintains close ties with its larger and more powerful neighbor. The two countries share a common cultural (religion, language, and many other aspects of their way of life) and tribal heritage. These ties were illustrated when the founder of Saudi Arabia, Ibn Saud, took refuge in Kuwait before he recaptured the city of Riyadh, today's Saudi capital.

One way of life that is disappearing in Kuwait is that of the country's Bedouin nomads. Their decline began in the early 1960s, when the government started to provide housing for rural dwellers. The Gulf War, which brought widespread

Very few Bedouin families still live in tents and maintain the nomadic liefestyle of their ancestors.

destruction to Kuwait's countryside, may have delivered the final blow to the Bedouin's age-old nomadic lifestyle. Not everyone born in Kuwait, or who has lived in Kuwait for centuries, is a citizen of the country. The Bedoons, which in Arabic means "without," are people who have no papers (documents) to prove their nationality; hence, they have no rights to citizenship. Many Bedoons are of Iraqi or Iranian ancestry but have lived in Kuwait for generations. Recently, Kuwait's ruler has made it possible for some Bedoons to become citizens of the country.

Ethnic and Social Divisions

Just as the population is changing, so is the ethnic distribution in Kuwait. In the early 1990s, the distribution of ethnic groups was as follows: Kuwaiti, 37 percent; non-Kuwaiti Arabs, 31 percent; and non-Arabs, 32 percent. Today, it is estimated that Kuwaitis make up 45 percent of the population;

non-Kuwait Arabs, 35 percent; and all others, 20 percent. The 'native' Kuwaitis who speak the Arabic language had a population of 886,400 in 1990. That population declined immediately after the Gulf War to about 700,000, but has now risen to about 815,200. Kuwait has five levels of society: the highest level is the ruling family; it is followed in stature by the old, wealthy, Kuwaiti merchant families; next are the former Bedouins who settled in Kuwait; the fourth level includes Arabs from other countries; and finally, there are the non-Arabic-speaking foreigners.

Languages

Arabic is Kuwait's official language. It is the language of government, business, media, and most personal communications. English is widely used in business, and is readily understood by many of the country's citizens, particularly those living in the larger cities. Arabic is taught in the schools, although there are several dialects spoken in Kuwait. The Kuwait dialect is a blend of southern Mesopotamia and peninsular Arabic, mixed with Persian, Indian, Egyptian, and English words. Street and shop signs are sometimes written in both English and Arabic. With a high literacy rate of nearly 80 percent, it is not surprising that there are seven daily newspapers. Two papers, the *Arab Times* and the *Kuwait Times,* are in English.

The Kuwaiti Arabs speak a form of Arabic commonly called "Gulf Arabic."

The words for counting from zero to ten are shown below.			
0	sifr	6	sitta
1	wahad	7	sabaa
2	ithnain	8	themanya
3	thalatha	9	tesaa
4	arbaaa	10	ashra
5	khamsa			

The following words or phrases would be useful if traveling in Kuwait.

my name	*isismi*
I don't understand	*Moo fahim*
hotel	*funduq*
embassy	*sifara*
money	*felous*
hospital	*mustashfa*
come	*taal*
go	*ruh*
give me	*atini*
bring	*yeeb*
yes	*sah*
no	*la*
good	*zain*
bad	*moo zain*
problem	*mishkula*
important	*muhimm*
police station	*makhfar*
brother	*akhooee*
sister	*ocktee*
quickly	*bih-surra*
come on	*yellah*
yesterday	*ams*
today	*al-youm*
tomorrow	*bachir*
here	*hini*
not here	*moo hihi*
later	*ba'dain*
God willing	*Inshallah*

Several daily newspapers keep the citizens of Kuwait up to date on national and international events.

Lifestyles

Kuwait's culture has been greatly influenced by the state religion. Islam (total submission to the will of God) is the official religion, and daily activity is to a large extent dependent on Islamic beliefs. The religion provides guidance for every aspect of life, including social, political, economic (commercial), and judicial. The origin of Islam and its beliefs and practices was discussed in chapter 3. Since more than 90 percent of all Kuwaitis are Muslims (followers of Islam), their culture is strongly influenced by the faith.

Muslim society is different from American society. For example, the Islamic calendar (Hijri) is based on the lunar year, which is 11 days shorter than the solar year on which the

These Kuwaiti men pray silently as part of the requirement that Muslims pray five times a day.

American (Christian) calendar is based. The Muslim day starts at sunrise and ends at sunset.

Kuwait's culture has been strongly influenced by several other factors. Being a desert nation, its strategic location on the Persian Gulf, and the discovery of oil in the early 20th century all have had a tremendous impact on the country's people, culture, and economy. Today, unlike many surrounding Arab nations, the Kuwaiti Arabs enjoy a modern and industrialized society. At times, however, the old values and ways of doing things conflict with the changes brought about by modernization and urban life.

Social Customs

Kuwaitis are hospitable and generous people. They are also conscious of honor and the family name. Reputation and respect are highly regarded. In other words, public behavior is important. Any individual public dishonor reflects on the person's family or group. Therefore, every effort is made to be conscious of one's public impressions in order not to be shamed. When one shows virtues, the person gains the respect of others. The long tradition of mixing with other cultures, as well as the teachings of the Islamic religion, may have caused the tradition of tolerance in Kuwait. Whether in individual family relations, or a much larger social setting, traditional virtues of hospitality, generosity, loyalty, and self-reliance are evident.

Cultural Tips

Each culture has its own traditions, or expected forms of behavior. Knowing in advance what some of the more important traditions are can save a visitor from being embarrassed. When visiting Kuwait, it is always best to ask for advice from your Kuwaiti friends or long-time residents. It shows respect for other cultures to know how to behave in certain situations and at certain times, such as during Ramadan, or the fasting period. Here are some cultural tips that visitors to Kuwait should know and practice.

- Be patient. Appointments and requests could be delayed if there are other more pressing needs or demands.

- Because of bureaucratic processes (government rules and procedures), getting things done often takes much longer in Kuwait than in the United States.

- Your word is honored, so do not expect all promises and or decisions to be in writing.

- You may be given an indirect answer, such as *Insha Allah* (God willing), to a question. This answer usually suggests a good intention by the person.

- It is advisable not to show signs of bad temper, talk loudly, or embarrass someone in a public place.

- Do not reject drinks when offered, as it is considered impolite. On the other hand, do not request alcoholic drinks, because they are forbidden by the Islamic faith.

- Be prepared to shake hands frequently. Also be aware that most Arabs sit, talk, and stand much closer than people in the West.

- And always remember: When in doubt, ask questions.

Family Structure

Family is the foundation of Kuwaiti society. A person does not represent just him or herself, but also the family and group from which the individual comes. As is true in other Arab lands, family honor is extremely important. Each member of the family has a defined role according to Arab tradition. The family provides security in times of economic hardship and in old age. The health, welfare, and happiness of family, friends, and strangers are important to the Kuwaiti Arab.

Under Islamic law, a man may have up to four wives. Getting married in Kuwait is financially rewarding, as the government provides a "marriage loan" to men marrying for the first time. When the couple has children, the government pays parents a monthly allowance for every child, with no limit to the number of children. This is one way the government hopes to increase the number of ethnic Kuwaitis in the country. As some Kuwaiti men study abroad, however, they often marry foreign women. This results in an increase in the number of unmarried Kuwaiti women.

A Kuwaiti Arab woman's first role is that of a wife and mother. Unlike many other Arab women, however, she does

A Kuwaiti woman is shown attending the opening of parliament in 1999, the same year that the National Assembly refused to grant women voting rights.

have a greater opportunity for independence. Kuwaiti Arab women have access to higher education, and many become teachers, businesswomen, and other professionals. Today, there are more women than men studying at Kuwait University. This opportunity has resulted in higher income not only for women, but also for the family. It is now possible for some women to hire other people to do the more traditional tasks, such as housekeeping.

Kuwaiti women are not allowed to vote. In 1999, the emir (ruler) issued a decree granting women the right to vote and to hold elected offices. But the National Assembly immediately struck down the ruling. Despite that shortcoming, women have many of the same rights as men. Women who hold key positions include Nabil al-Mulla, who as Kuwait's ambassador to Australia was the first female to hold such a position; Fayza al-Khorafi, who became the first female rector of an Arab university (in 1993); and Rasha al-Sabah, who became under secretary of higher education.

Souk (Market)

One of the most interesting places to visit in Kuwait or any other Arab country is the *souk* (market), or *bakala* (grocery market). Nearly every kind of food available in American or European groceries can be purchased in Kuwait. Most of these items are imported, however, and their prices are generally higher than in their country of origin.

Several modern supermarkets exist in Kuwait. And each district has a cooperative supermarket, where prices tend to be lower than in the privately owned supermarkets. Some co-ops are open 24 hours. The souks are bigger and operate from 7:30 A.M. until noon on weekdays, and from 4:00 P.M. to 9:00 P.M. every day except Friday, which is the day of prayer for Muslims. Souks are wonderful places to visit. A great variety of items are available for purchase, ranging from Kuwaiti doors to Bedouin coffeepots, and Persian carpets to fine gold jewelry. Modern shopping malls also are becoming popular, with at least one in each of the larger cities.

Food

Traditional Kuwait dishes often consist of rice prepared in various ways; *fuul*, a paste made from beans, garlic, and lemon served in oil; falafel, deep-fried balls of chickpea paste with spices served with flat bread (*khobz*); and hummus, a paste made with pureed chickpeas, lemon, sesame paste, oil, and spices. A main dish will contain chicken, meat (but not pork), or fish. Arabic flat bread is usually served at all meals. There are some foreign restaurants, including those offering Indian cuisine that features spicy rice dishes. Recently, American fast food restaurants have opened almost everywhere in Kuwait.

Clothing

All types of clothing are available from the souks. Adult clothing from Europe is sold in boutiques and can be quite expensive. Garments imported from India, Morocco (Africa), Turkey, Thailand, and Taiwan are much less expensive. Men's clothes are less expensive than women's clothes, but there are fewer selections. One can buy fabric from both the *salmiya* (cotton) souk and the central souk. Tailors are available to sew the fabric into a pattern of choice. Most of the tailors/seamstresses in the country are from Pakistan or India, and they are quite inexpensive.

There are three modes of dressing in Kuwait: Western, traditional, and Islamic. Many professionals now wear Western clothing. Even in Kuwait's hot climate, suits and ties are commonplace. Traditional clothing for men includes the floor length white cotton robe that is usually worn over a loose, pajama type of pants. A similar garment suited to colder weather is made of wool. Headwear is called *gahfiya*, which consists of a small, round, knitted cap covered by a bigger piece of cloth, the usually white *khitra*. The above two pieces of clothing are secured in place with an *igal* (cord). Occasionally, men also wear a *bisht* (coat or cloak) over the traditional *dishdasha*, or long robe.

The women wear *dara'a*, a loose-fitting dress that comes in different colors. They are usually decorated with bright colorful embroideries with gold threads. Women also wear ankle-length skirts with blouses, particularly when they go to work or school. The Islamic dress involves the use of veils called *hijab*. The veil is worn over a silky black gown (cloak) that flows from head to toe. This is worn over the traditional dress. A light sheer transparent black garment, used for dancing, and *burqa* and *bushiya* are other types of veils.

Kuwait City offers shoppers different styles of clothing. Kuwaitis dress in Western, traditional, or Islamic styles.

Not every Muslim agrees that women must continue to wear veils. Citing the Qur'an, however, there are three codes that prescribe women's dress. The first rule is that of what forms the best garment: "O children of Adam, we have provided you with garments to cover your bodies, as well as for luxury. But the best garment is the garment of righteousness. These are some of God's signs, that they may take heed." (Qur'an 7:26). The second rule is that of covering the breasts: "And tell the believing women to subdue their eyes, and maintain their chastity. They shall not reveal any parts of their bodies, except that which is necessary. They shall cover their chests, (with their Khimar) and shall not relax this code in the presence of other than their husbands, their fathers, the father of their husbands, their sons, the sons of their husbands, their brothers, the sons of their brothers, the sons of sisters, other women, the male servants or employees whose sexual drive has been nullified, or the children who have not reached puberty." (Qur'an 24:31; Khalifa's translation). The third rule sets the length of garments, "O Prophet, tell your wives, your daughters, and wives of the believers that they shall lengthen their garments. Thus, they will be recognized and avoid being insulted." (Qur'an 33:59) Women, today and in Kuwait, are no longer forced to abide by these dress codes. But modesty, religion, and tradition continue to dictate that women dress modestly when in public places.

In June 1999 former member of parliament Mubarak al-Duwaila held a meeting with voters before the July parliamentary elections. The winners of the election served in the 50-seat National Assembly.

6

Government

K uwait became an independent nation on June 19, 1961, when it obtained its independence from Great Britain. Before this date, Kuwait was an independent state under the protection of the British. The "modern" Kuwait began in the mid-1700s with the installation of the Sabah as its leader. Today, over 250 years later, the country is still governed by the Sabah family.

Appointment of Leaders

The government has been described as a constitutional monarchy, governed by the Al-Sabah family. Some people believe Kuwait is a welfare state because the government provides free housing and many other social services for its citizens. The current ruler (emir) of Kuwait is His Highness Sheik Jaber al-Ahmad al-Jaber al-Sabah. The sheik, the hereditary monarch of the Mubarak line of the ruling

Al-Sabah family, serves as head of state. A prime minister is appointed by the sheik to head the government. The emir's successor, the crown prince and prime minister, is His Highness Sheik Saad al-Abdullah al-Salim al-Sabah. The emir selects his successor, the crown prince, in consultation with the ruling family as is stipulated by the constitution. The crown prince who becomes the prime minister, the head of govern-ment, is then confirmed by parliament.

In other words, one can only become the head of state if one is born into the Al-Sabah family. The emir rules with help from his appointed ministers, most of whom are his relatives. The Sabah family holds key ministerial positions (finance, defense, oil, and foreign affairs), including that of the prime minister—the individual who actually heads the government.

Decision Making

At the grass-roots level, many decisions are made at *diwaniya* (pronounced dee-wahn-ee-ya) meetings—a social gathering usually held weekly. This custom goes back many centuries and has roots in the customs of tribal societies. The diwaniya is a type of "family" (extended family, clan, neighborhood) meeting where members may discuss or debate what is going on in the government. Politics and other business are discussed at these meetings. The group leader forwards decisions made at these meetings to higher authorities. Often, men may attend several different diwaniyas. At each of these meetings ideas are discussed and, if agreed upon, they are passed on to higher level diwaniyas, until eventually they reach the ruling body. In this way, everyone feels that they at least have a say in the political process. The system allows at least a form of democracy to prevail in this country where varied opinions are listened to and often valued. This system, for example, was at least partly responsible for the firm resistance offered by Kuwaitis during the Iraqi invasion (Gulf War).

Ultimately, the emir makes most major decisions. He rules, or exercises his power, through a cabinet called the Council of Ministers. This decision-making body is headed by the prime minister who is also the crown prince. Kuwait also has an elected parliament known as Majlis al-Umma (the National Assembly). There are 50 members of parliament (MPs) who are elected by popular vote by their wards (voting areas where they live). Political parties do not exist in Kuwait, but campaigns are conducted on an individual basis through the diwaniya system. Though no formal political parties exist, political groups abound. Among the more influential political groups are the Kuwait Democratic Forum (KDF), the National Democratic group, the Islamic National Alliance, the Islamic Constitutional Movement (ICM), the Tribal Confederation, and the Independence Party.

The emir can dissolve the parliament whenever he sees fit to do so. Tensions occasionally arise between the parliament and the emir, even though he appointed most ministers to their posts. On occasion, the emir has closed parliament, as happened in 1976, 1986, and 1999, because of some dispute. It should be noted that the 1999 closing followed the appearance of the country's revised constitution. Dissension occurred because the revision allows the parliament to veto legislation proposed by the emir. The parliamentarians, or assembly members, are accountable to the entire nation and not only to their constituents.

Constitution

The Kuwait Constitution is the primary document establishing rules by which the country is governed. The emir (Amir) signed the country's original constitution into law on November 11, 1962. The document, containing 83 Articles, has American (presidential), British (parliamentary), and Arabic (Islamic) elements. The first six articles shown below set the stage for the state and the system of government

Kuwaiti men are shown waiting to vote at a polling place.

(state control, religion, language, the ruler, the emblem, and the type of government).

Article One

Kuwait is an independent sovereign Arab State. Neither its sovereignty nor any part of its territory may be relinquished. The people of Kuwait are a part of the Arab Nation.

Article Two

The religion of the State is Islam, and the Islamic Sharia shall be a main source of legislation.

Article Three

The official language of the State is Arabic.

Article Four

Kuwait is a hereditary Emirate, the succession to which shall be in the descendants of the late Mubarak al-Sabah.

The Heir Apparent shall be designated within one year, at the latest, from the date of accession of the Amir.

His designation shall be effected by an Amiri Order upon the nomination of the Amir and the approval of the National Assembly, which shall be signified by a majority vote of its members in a special sitting.

In case no designation is achieved in accordance with the foregoing procedure, the Amir shall nominate at least three of the descendants of the late Mubarak al-Sabah of whom the National Assembly shall pledge allegiance to one as Heir Apparent.

The Heir Apparent shall have attained his majority, be of sound mind and a legitimate son of Muslim parents.

A special law promulgated within one year from the date of coming into force of this Constitution shall lay down the other rules of succession in the Emirate. The said law shall be of a constitutional nature and therefore shall be capable of amendment only by the procedure prescribed for amendment of the Constitution.

Article Five

The flag, emblem, badges, decorations and National Anthem of the State shall be specified by law.

Article Six

The System of Government in Kuwait shall be democratic, under which sovereignty resides in the people, the source of all powers. Sovereignty shall be exercised in the manner specified in this Constitution.

Article four of the constitution defines Kuwait as a hereditary emirate with succession limited to descendants of Sheik Mubarak al-Sabah only. The constitution does not allow

"When will Kuwaiti women get their political and social rights to vote and [run for office]?" That is the question posed by these women activists in Kuwait in 2002.

women to vote, and a decree issued by the emir on May 16, 1999, allowing women to vote was struck down by the National Assembly in November 1999. Only a change in the constitution will allow women to vote and to hold elected public offices.

The constitution is divided into several sections and part III addresses the matter of public rights and duties. This part of the constitution guarantees various human rights and freedoms, such as freedom from arbitrary arrest, the right to a fair trial, and freedom of religion, speech, and the press. This section also guarantees freedom of association and freedom of private and public meetings. It should be noted that some of these freedoms are subject to "conditions and manner specified by law."

Governorship/Legislature

The emir is the head of state; therefore, Kuwait is an emirate. A crown prince is the prime minister, that is, the head of government. The emir is vested with legislative power along with the National Assembly. According to the constitution, the assembly is made up of 50 members, who are to be "elected directly by universal suffrage and secret ballot" with a four-year term limit. The emir, the ministers, or the assembly may initiate legislation. In order for legislation to become law, it must be officially made known and supported by the emir, and published in *Al-Youm*, the official gazette.

To ease the task of governing the country, Kuwait is divided into five states, or governorates. They are Kuwait City (the capital), Hawalli (Hawally), Jahra, Farwaniya, and Ahmadi. A governor administers each of the five regional units. At a still smaller level, there is a branch of government known as the Municipality, which is overseen by the elected Municipal Council. This branch of government is responsible for urban planning. Their jobs include cleaning, collection of garbage, inspection of food and restaurants, and issuing building permits in Kuwait City and the suburbs.

Sharing the Wealth

As has been mentioned on several previous occasions, Kuwait is a constitutional monarchy, ruled by the Al-Sabah family for more than 250 years. The current ruler—His Highness, Emir Sheik Jaber al-Ahmad al-Jaber al-Sabah—is the 13th ruler of the Al-Sabah dynasty. During his rule, Kuwait's oil resources have brought the country tremendous wealth. The emir decided to establish a welfare system that allows all citizens to benefit from the country's prosperity.

All citizens of Kuwait receive government-subsidized housing, education, and health services. Subsidized housing, first provided in the early 1960s, virtually eliminated the nomadic Bedouin lifestyle. Rural housing was built with enclosed yards for the nomads' animals, so officially Kuwait no longer has a nomadic population or culture.

Every Kuwaiti wants to own a private home. Despite more than 40 years of government involvement in providing adequate housing, problems still exist. Officially, there are no homeless people in the country. New housing units are almost always under construction. Currently, work is underway on housing that will accommodate another 600,000 citizens. Government housing is made available to all married Kuwaitis at a nominal monthly rent if they are employed and do not own property. In addition, the occupants receive an income of 100 Kuwaiti dinar (about three hundred U.S. dollars) per month if they are not employed.

Currency

Kuwait's currency is the Kuwaiti dinar (KD), and there are 1,000 fils to the dinar. It is effectively pegged to the U.S. dollar, the currency in which most of the world's oil is traded, and in which Kuwait is paid for its exports. Kuwait's currency can be exchanged for any other foreign currency. The exchange rates are posted daily in the newspapers and are available through the automated telephone answering systems of some banks.

Social Services

Several establishments, including the ministries of public health, education, social affairs, and labor, provide free social services to the citizens. The Ministry of Public Health has one of the best and most developed health-care services in the world. Medical treatment is offered free to all citizens. There are 27 hospitals in the country, 17 government run and 10 that offer private care. Most of them have state-of-the-art medical technology and equipment. Well-trained physicians and other health-care professionals staff them. There are more than 3,200 government doctors and several hundred doctors in private practice.

Education

In Kuwait, "Education is a right . . . guaranteed by the state in accordance with law and within the limits of public policy and morals. Education in its preliminary stages shall be

Women and men, such as those shown here at Kuwait University, are educated in the same classrooms at the university level.

compulsory and free in accordance with law" (Article 40 of the Kuwait Constitution). The Ministry of Education provides free education from kindergarten through the university level, and even offers scholarships to students who wish to study abroad. Most of the schools are government owned and the language of instruction is Arabic. Education in the country is patterned on the American and British systems, incorporating practices of both. Schooling is compulsory for all Kuwaitis between the ages of 6 and 14. Youngsters cannot be legally employed until they reach age 15. Boys and girls go to separate schools.

The country has private schools, many of which are American or British operated. Many foreigners living in Kuwait attend these schools in which English is the language of instruction. Private schools in Kuwait are still subject to state rules governing education; that is, they are under the jurisdiction of the Ministry of Education. Some Kuwaiti families send their children to these private schools. This is particularly true of students who are preparing to attend college in Europe or North America.

Nearly 80 percent of Kuwait's people are literate. This is a high rate for a Middle Eastern country. Both women and men receive a free education through the university level. The country offers about 80 kindergartens, 180 primary schools, 145 secondary schools, and one university. There are also 11 institutes of postsecondary vocational training and a Maintenance Training Center that teach courses on electronics, machine tools, diesel and gasoline engines, and air-conditioning. The government and Kuwait University sponsor 140 adult literacy centers. Here, adults who are unable to read or write receive free instruction in the hope of raising the country's literacy rate even higher. Kuwait University also provides a variety of classes for adults who simply want to further their education without working toward a college degree. Institutes of special education that cater to the needs of the disabled are also available.

Other Services

The Ministries of Social Affairs and Labor, through their various institutions, care for children, youth, and the disabled. They also provide financial aid to families in need and offer social care for laborers and elderly citizens. All government and public institutions support the Social Securities Authority, which, as in the United States, is concerned with matters relating to retirement pensions and compensation paid in cases of sickness and death.

Oil. With the discovery of oil, Anglo-Persian Oil of Great Britain and Gulf Oil Corporation of America formed an operating unit called the Kuwait Oil Company (KOC) in 1934. In 1938, a large oil field was discovered in the Burgan area that increased the country's oil revenues. Kuwait's oil reserves rank fourth in the world. Even though production was seriously curtailed during the Gulf War, the country continues to rank among the world's major producers. When its oil fields are in full production, Kuwait's per capita gross national product ranks at or near the world's highest. The importance of this precious resource is clearly illustrated by the fact that oil revenues account for more than 90 percent of the country's total income. It is this wealth that makes so many government services possible.

Sea Ports. Al-Shuwaikh, Al-Shuaiba, and Doha are the three main seaports in Kuwait. Al-Shuwaikh is the largest and oldest of the three ports, and it was established in 1960.

Air Transportation. Kuwait has one international airport. It is located southwest of Kuwait City. The airport was seriously damaged during the Iraqi invasion in 1990. Kuwait International Airport has been rebuilt and updated and now meets international standards. It has the latest and most sophisticated equipment, facilities, and services, including automated flight information monitors, banking, restaurants, a mosque, taxis and car rental services, hotel reservations, a duty-free shopping center, and a transit airport hotel. Kuwait has one airline—Kuwait Airways Corporation (KAC)—that was established in 1954 and is half owned by the government.

Even though Kuwait's system of government seems strange by Western standards, it works. The people have many freedoms, and some voice in the way their country is run. They prosper and enjoy one of the region's highest standards of living.

Oil is the source of Kuwait's wealth. This refinery contributes to the large amount of oil produced by this small country.

7

Economy

A t first glance, Kuwait may not appear to be endowed with many valuable natural resources, especially land. It is, after all, a rather harsh desert land that is dotted with very few oases. There are no lakes or rivers; there is very little soil; vegetation is sparse, as is animal life; and there are no metal resources. Yet it is one of the world's richest countries and the wealth is based on a single natural resource—"black gold," or petroleum. This chapter discusses Kuwait's resources and other aspects of the country's strong economy.

Water

Water is the most precious natural resource in any desert area. Kuwait has no permanent surface water. Dry streambeds flow only briefly after a period of rain; natural depressions accumulate rainwater after storms, but it is gone in a matter of days or weeks.

A small portion of this temporary surface water seeps into the ground, but most of it is lost to evaporation. Such groundwater as exists may be fresh. These freshwater springs or wells are the sites of oases—places in a desert where good water is available for drinking, other domestic uses, watering animals, and perhaps irrigating crops. In many places, however, the groundwater is brackish (somewhat salty) and of little use.

Kuwait's freshwater resources cannot supply even a small fraction of the country's needs. Because of the scarcity of fresh water, the country relies on seawater desalinization (removing salt from water). Huge desalinization plants take water from the Persian Gulf, remove the salts and other impurities, and produce nearly all of the country's freshwater supply. The country has six of these plants, the first having been built in 1953. All the plants combined produce 33,554,000 cubic feet (950,000 cubic meters) of water per day. The country also treats and recovers its wastewater. About 80 to 90 percent of all wastewater—more than 4 trillion cubic feet (113 million cubic meters)—is treated and reused for irrigation of crops and landscaping.

Agriculture

Kuwait's inadequate water supply is a major limiting factor for agriculture. So is the lack of abundant good soil. Rock surfaces, salty deposits, barren sand, or surfaces destroyed by oil pollution during the Gulf War cover most of the country. Cropland covers less than 1 percent of Kuwait's total land area. Major crops include alfalfa hay, vegetables, potatoes, and other foods for human consumption.

Where farming is practiced, crops are irrigated with wastewater. The government heavily subsidizes the cost of water. Irrigation started in Kuwait in the 1950s. Originally, the system used a network of surface canals to run water across fields. Later, sprinkler irrigation was introduced. A still more recent introduction is the micro-irrigation system in greenhouses. About 11,787 acres (4,770 hectares) of land are now cultivated using this method. There are generally three types of farms—those privately owned, those belonging to institutions, and those owned by companies.

Most farmland is located near the coast. Some problems are beginning to occur as a result of irrigating the land. In some places, salt is accumulating in the soil at a fast rate, making it unfit for crops. In other areas, particularly those where soil has a high clay content, water has started to collect in a process called water logging. In both cases, soil becomes ruined and unable to produce crops.

Focus on the Sea

The Persian Gulf has long been a major resource for Kuwait. Centuries before the discovery of oil in Kuwait, the country's economy was based on seafaring trade. Its excellent natural harbor and strategic location between the west and the east made Kuwait an important trade route in ancient times. Later, during the 19th and early 20th centuries, the economy shifted to pearl diving and people invested in Kuwait's pearl banks.

Pearls are valuable gems that form naturally in mollusks, particularly oysters. And vast oyster beds litter the floor of the Persian Gulf in the vicinity of Kuwait. For centuries, pearl divers have risked their lives to gather mollusks from the seafloor. When a diver's basket was filled with mollusks, he returned to the surface. Shells were then opened in the hope of finding the small, precious gems. Pearls can have different colors, but most are whitish. They are used to make jewelry, particularly necklaces, ring settings, and earrings.

In the 1930s three things happened to all but destroy the Persian Gulf pearling industry. First, the global financial depression destroyed the market; most people simply could no longer afford to buy luxury items. A second blow came from Japan, where a process was developed to cultivate pearls, or create them under artificial, rather than natural, conditions. The process involves inserting a tiny grain of sand into a

The Persian Gulf provides an income for fishermen and food for Kuwaitis.

mollusk. The shellfish then secretes a fluid called nacre in order to prevent irritation by the sand. The nacre then hardens into a pearl. Finally, Kuwait began producing oil. Many people gave up the difficult job of pearling for safer, easier, and often more dependable employment in the petroleum industry.

Pearl diving went hand-in-hand with boat building in Kuwait. Boat building was a lucrative business. When the pearl diving season (May to September) was over, traders used the boats for long-distance commerce. Kuwaitis gained a reputation for making boats from the most durable materials and of the highest quality. A few privileged families strictly controlled both the pearl diving and boat building industries. While they made huge fortunes, the general public gained little from either activity—other than income provided by their contribution of labor.

Fishing was another industry that relied on resources from

the gulf. Although it never gained the importance of pearl diving or boat building, it did provide a valuable source of food. The gulf has dozens of varieties of edible fish and other forms of marine life. Fishing is still an important economic activity, and seafood remains an important part of the Kuwaiti diet. Coral reefs lying off Kuwait's shore add still another potentially valuable marine resource. Their beauty makes them well worth seeing, hence, a potential tourist attraction.

Petroleum

For centuries, desert nomads had noticed a strange, black, foul-smelling, thick liquid oozing out of the ground. It was not until the 1930s, however, that the importance of this resource was recognized and it began to be tapped. Drilling for oil began in Kuwait in 1936 by the Kuwait Oil Company. Kuwait Oil was a cooperative venture owned by the Anglo-Persian Oil Company of Great Britain and Gulf Oil, an American firm. Commercial export of the crude oil started in 1946, immediately after World War II. Eventually, other companies were allowed in to drill in different parts of the country.

Kuwait's government now owns the Kuwait Oil Company, which is now called the Kuwait Petroleum Corporation, having purchased all shares formerly held by foreign interests. This new, huge, government-owned corporation now controls all oil related activities in the country—including prospecting for oil, drilling, refining, distribution, and trade.

Oil Resources

Kuwait has one of the most productive oil fields in the world. Its Burqua field is the second largest in the world, exceeded only by the huge Saudi Arabian Ghawar field. Other major fields in Kuwait include Sabriyah, Al-Wafrah, and Umm-Gudair. Today, Kuwait's oil resources contribute about 90 percent of the nation's total income.

The country currently produces about two million barrels

of oil daily. Its oil reserves are estimated to be approximately 100 million barrels—giving the country about 8 to 9 percent of the worldwide total. In oil production, figures can change from year to year. Over a period of several decades, Kuwait's production ranks fifth. This is a tremendous amount of oil to be produced by a country as small as Kuwait and with a population just over two million. Kuwait consumes about 9 percent of all the oil it produces and exports the rest.

In the past, natural gas has been burned (flared) as a waste product of oil production. Increasingly, however, Kuwait is developing its natural gas resources. Rather than burning the gas in the oilfields, it is now being used. Much of the gas is used to generate electricity.

Economic Diversification

It is dangerous for any country to depend almost exclusively on a single resource or industry for most of its economic well being. Kuwait realizes that its economy must become much more diversified, that it cannot depend forever on its petroleum reserves. During recent years, diversification has become a government priority. Some of the diversification is oil based, such as in petrochemical industries and fertilizer manufacturing plants. Kuwait has also invested in food processing and salt manufacturing plants. Other investments included fabrication of building materials and other construction materials. Kuwait also realizes that an investment in its own people is the most important investment any government can make. The government continues to improve its already solid education and health-care programs to further develop the country's human resources.

Management

With its oil wealth, Kuwait is able to give its people one of the world's most comprehensive social, educational, and health and welfare packages. Keeping these important programs going, however, requires the government to manage its financial resources properly. It must also plan ahead, to a time when oil revenue will decline. The government has begun to put funds aside to ensure that future generations of Kuwaitis receive similar benefits.

Kuwait's economy declined during the Iran-Iraq war of the 1980s. While this conflict was underway, a number of restrictions brought trade between Kuwait and its two warring neighbors to a standstill. It was the 1990 Gulf War and its aftermath, however, which almost wrecked the country's economy. Transportation was devastated, cities lay in ruin, communications were largely destroyed, and the oil industry (literally) went up in flames. Losses from the Gulf War amounted to over $170 billion—and this figure does not include the much greater cost of damage to oil wells or other oil-related installations.

By 1998 the Kuwaiti economy had rebounded, recording a gross national product (GNP) of $58.6 billion. To reduce its dependence on oil, the government continues to work on diversifying the economy. This effort on the government's part includes expansion of the petrochemical and fertilizer industries.

With wealth and modernization comes the need for modern gadgets such as color television, washing machines, sound systems, and computers. But these modern necessities rely on electricity to run or function. Each year, Kuwaitis increase their use of electricity by 5 percent. The country is having some difficulty keeping up with the rapidly growing demand for electrical energy. To meet the challenge, a new electrical plant was opened in 2000, and several other power plants are either planned or being studied for the country's future. New plants are powered by natural gas, which, in turn, produces electrical energy.

Wealthy Kuwaitis

Kuwait's financial reserves were depleted following the Gulf War. However, with a strong showing of oil in the world market, the government now has surplus money that it is

The Kuwait Stock Exchange is where traders watch oil prices. In 1982, Kuwait suffered a stock market crash that had a significant impact on the economy.

investing in an account called the Fund for Future Generations. In 1999 the country had a gross domestic product (GDP) of $42 billion. With a population of approximately two million, the per capita GDP rose above $22,000—making Kuwait one of the world's wealthiest nations.

Transportation

The country has a total of 2,914 miles (4,700 kilometers) of well-maintained roads. About three-quarters of the roads are paved, with the rest being gravel, or unpaved. Most of the roads are found in the more heavily populated eastern part of the country, near the coast.

Kuwait's international airport is located southwest of Kuwait City. There is only one national carrier, Kuwait Airways. Kuwait's seaports handle petroleum exports and commercial imports. Kuwait exports most of its oil by ship to Japan and other Asian countries. It also exports oil to several European countries and to the United States. About 4 percent of U.S. oil imports come from Kuwait.

Banking and Finance

The Indian rupee was the currency used before Kuwait gained independence in 1961. Since then, its own currency, the dinar, has been introduced and used. The Kuwait Central Bank issues five different currency notes. One Kuwait dinar is worth about three U.S. dollars.

Future Economy Trend

Kuwait has faced three major economic problems during recent decades. The first was the long war between Iran and Iraq during the 1980s, which restricted trade between Kuwait and those two nations. The second setback was the 1982 stock market crash, which resulted in some $19 billion worth of checks becoming valueless. The third problem was the Gulf War, a tragedy that depleted the financial resources of the country. This conflict seriously damaged, or destroyed, much of the infrastructure—things like roads, airports, power networks, oil refineries, oil wells, desalinization plants, and port facilities. Damage from the Gulf War alone is estimated to have been about $170 billion. The environmental impact of the Gulf War is the subject of the next chapter.

Fires burned in oil wells and refineries after Iraq attacked Kuwait. A worker is shown here pausing for midday prayers as a fire burns near Kuwait City in 1991.

8

The Gulf War

D uring its history, Kuwait has been involved in several wars. It is located in a turbulent part of the world in which conflicts are commonplace. Before the region had well-defined nations like Iran, Iraq, Saudi Arabia, and Kuwait itself, there had been many hostilities between the Persians and Arabs along the Persian Gulf's west coast. Nebuchadnezzar and Alexander the Great are some of the better-known people who ruled the area in ancient times. The Romans also dominated this region at one time. Because of its strategic location and importance to trade, many powers sought to control the gulf. When Islam was added to the cultural and religious mix, additional conflict was created. Finally, during the 20th century, the region's vast oil wealth provided additional fuel for the fires of conflict.

In chapter 3, the many close links between Kuwait and neighboring

Iraq were discussed at length. Both were at one time part of the Ottoman Empire, and their regional rulers were sometimes based in Iraq. More than once, attempts were made to more completely dominate, or to even conquer, Kuwait.

What was the cause of these wars? There is no single answer to this question, but the main reasons are either economic or political. Iraq has had border disputes with Kuwait that began during the Ottoman Empire period. In 1913 the British drafted a document recognizing Ottoman rule over Kuwait. But simultaneously, the British declared Kuwait to be an independent country within the Ottoman Empire. This document was not signed before World War I started. The Ottoman Empire was ended by the events of World War I, and soon thereafter (1923 Treaty of Lausanne) Turkey renounced all claims to former Ottoman regions. At this time, Iraq claimed Kuwait as part of its territory. But the British did not sanction this claim, because they still had some control over Kuwait.

Iraq agreed to the location of a boundary between itself and Kuwait when it applied to become a member of the League of Nations in 1932. This agreement was short lived, however, when large reserves of oil were discovered in Kuwait. Also at this time, there was a power struggle going on in Kuwait between the ruling Sabah family and several other powerful families. Iraq attempted to use this internal disturbance in Kuwait—known as the Majlis Movement—to expand its borders. The Majlis Movement failed to topple the ruling government, however, and Iraq was unsuccessful in its attempt to gain control of Kuwait.

Iraq made another attempt to annex its small neighbor after Kuwait had gained its full independence as a nation in 1961. However, when a new ruler came to power in Iraq, the government agreed to recognize Kuwait's sovereignty. This led to a better relationship between the two nations, who agreed to accept the existing border drawn in 1932. But border tensions did continue between the two nations over Warbah and the

Iraqi cavalry soldiers paraded in Baghdad as part of the preparations by Iraq to invade Kuwait in 1961.

Bubiyan islands. On August 2, 1990, however, an event occurred that totally changed the fragile relationship that existed between Kuwait and Iraq. Kuwait was invaded by Iraq in an attempt to occupy and annex Kuwait. The resulting conflict is known as the Gulf War.

The primary underlying reason for Iraq's invasion was economic. Iraq needed cash. Even though the country is a major oil producer, its revenue had been depleted by its long and costly war with Iran. Iraq accused Kuwait of producing more oil than it was allowed by the Organization of the Petroleum Exporting Countries (OPEC). Iraq believed that the world price of oil was much lower than it should be due to Kuwait's flooding of the market with its petroleum exports. Iraq, its government reasoned, was not getting a fair price for its oil. The Iraqis also wanted Kuwait to forgive a debt of about $13 billion it owed Kuwait, resulting from the Iran-Iraq war (1980-1988). The combined political and economic disputes between the two countries resulted in Iraq's decision to invade Kuwait on August 2, 1990. Within days,

Iraq had annexed Kuwait. Kuwait immediately sought help from the United Nations, and the Gulf War began.

The War

Before the invasion of Kuwait, the Iraqi leader, President Saddam Hussein, stated his goal of uniting all Arab lands by eliminating artificial political boundaries. He also said that he intended to redistribute wealth in the region. Hussein explained his plan to distribute the wealth currently held by leaders of the oil-rich gulf states to Arabs in the poorer Arab countries once the artificial boundaries were eliminated. He also renewed the old claim that Kuwait was historically part of Iraq under the Ottoman Empire.

The gulf area is very important to the rest of the world because of its huge oil reserves. If Iraq successfully controlled Kuwait, it would have control over nearly 20 percent of the world's known oil reserves. There was great concern in the West that the Gulf War could destabilize the entire area. Iraq planned to fully annex Kuwait after the invasion. Attempts to negotiate a peaceful settlement by several of the region's Arab governments failed. The international communities immediately intervened, first by bringing economic sanctions against Iraq. The United Nations Security Council also passed several resolutions, none of which Iraq heeded.

This led to a meeting of the United Nations Security Council on November 19, 1990. Iraq was given an ultimatum to withdraw its forces from Kuwait by the middle of January 1991. Failure by Iraq would lead to measures necessary to enforce the resolution. The United States, under then-President George H. Bush, attempted to mediate the conflict by scheduling several meetings between the U.S. secretary of state and Iraq's foreign minister. Meetings were held, but Iraq refused to back down. In fact, the Iraqis further clouded the issue— in hope of gaining support of other Muslim dominated states—by linking the invasion to other issues such as the

These U.S. soldiers were deployed across the Saudi desert to fight in Kuwait during the Gulf War.

Arab Palestinian-Israeli affair. The secretary general of the United Nations made still another attempt to get the Iraqis to withdraw. They were asked to leave Kuwait by January 15, 1991. Again, Iraq held firm.

A military coalition led by the United States went to war over Kuwait on January 17, 1991. There are, of course, differing accounts of what happened—simply because people from different countries and cultures saw the event from different perspectives. Iraqi forces were no match for those of the coalition. Air strikes destroyed most of Iraq's strategic installations. Once they were destroyed, ground troops entered the fray. Within six weeks, Iraq was defeated. On February 26, 1991, President Saddam Hussein renounced his claim to Kuwait. He also agreed to the conditions set up by the United Nations, including restitution (payments) for war damage caused in Kuwait.

Postwar

One outcome of the Gulf War was the visible division among the Arab nations. Forty percent of the Arab nations supported Iraq's claims and effort. But the majority of Arab nations were strongly opposed to Iraq's invasion of Kuwait. This distrust of one another among some Arab nations is not only noticeable at the governmental level; it is also evident among many Arab people.

Politics

Some political opposition to the ruling family was expressed as a result of the Gulf War. A number of citizens were opposed to the way the government was being operated. In the constitution, only someone from the Al-Sabah family can be the emir of Kuwait. The Sabah family members still occupy key government positions, such as those of the prime minister, foreign affairs minister, and finance minister. Some Kuwaitis resent the fact that only members of the ruling family can govern the country. These dissenting groups seek a more democratic government and society. A few groups, on the other hand, believe that the government is not tough enough. They would like to see the ruling family be even more autocratic, particularly those opposing the "westernization" of Kuwait.

Long-time antagonists became unified during the Gulf

War in voicing their demand for a more open and democratic government. One condition sought by the dissenting group was to gain the right to elect members of the National Assembly. They believed that elected members of the National Assembly would provide a good check on the cabinet and the ruling family's authority. The emir agreed to the election of members for the National Council, thereby making Kuwait one of the most democratic Persian Gulf states.

War and the Economy

When the Iraqi soldiers retreated from occupied Kuwait, they sabotaged the country's economy. Much of the infrastructure, including oil wells, refineries, and desalinization plants were destroyed. Its economy did benefit in one way, however. Trade increased greatly because of the need to replace or rebuild what had been destroyed. Many high paying jobs were created in the construction sector of the economy.

The Gulf War was also supposed to give the government an opportunity to attain a Kuwaiti ethnic majority in the country (ethnic Kuwaitis number well under half of the nation's population). During the conflict, many foreign workers fled. The government could not carry out its restrictive policies, however, because Kuwait depended on foreign laborers to fill many of the essential jobs. Prior to their departure, foreigners had done much of the highly technical work. The essential oil and banking industries, in particular, relied heavily on foreign expertise. Kuwait had to train its nationals to take over some of those vacancies left open by the foreigners.

When Iraqi troops pulled out, they set on fire more than 700 oil wells, and also destroyed many other key facilities for oil production. Restoring these functions became an immediate—and very expensive—task. The oil industry was given high priority after the war because it is the country's main source of revenue. The oil production, refining, and export industries had to return to full capacity as soon as possible to generate the revenue required to repair and restore the economy. The cost of reconstruction was in excess of $20 billion.

Security

Security became a major issue for Kuwait after the Gulf War. In the past, Kuwait had always been prudent and shrewd in its dealing with Arab and non-Arab neighbors. But with the war, things changed. The government now has its own larger and more powerful armed forces. Although the country has always had its own military, after the Gulf War there were major changes in the way the armed forces were structured.

The country has three branches of armed forces. This is significant considering its small population. Before the war, the military was not highly respected by the Kuwaitis. Wages were low, and military life was looked down upon. Morale was low among those serving in the military. In an attempt to recruit enough people for its armed forces, the government recently mandated a type of national service for all able citizens 18 years and above.

Prior to the Gulf War, security was of some concern to people of the gulf states. Five gulf states—Bahrain, Kuwait, Oman, Qatar, and United Arab Emirates—joined with Saudi Arabia in 1981 to form the Gulf Cooperation Council. Their aim was to form a defensive military alliance. This alliance came as a result of the war between Iran and Iraq. There was fear that if Iranians defeated the Iraqis, there would be more trouble in the region. In Iran, Shiite Muslims hold power, whereas Sunnis are the majority in all other Gulf Sates, including Saudi Arabia. The alliance was to form a collective system of self-defense that would not need to call upon foreign military powers for help. Ultimately, however, not only Kuwait, but other gulf states as well, turned to the West to develop better security strategies for the region.

The strategic location of Kuwait and the other coastal gulf

In 1998, then Kuwaiti Defense Minister Sheik Salim al-Sabah (right with headdress) visited with the Kuwaiti Army near the border of Iraq.

states placed them in a position making them vulnerable to attack. They also had a limited military capability. Kuwait was somewhat protected to the south and west—at least from ground attack—by the vast surrounding desert. But to the north, across its land boundary with Iraq, there was no natural line of defense.

Kuwait's military was almost completely destroyed by the

Iraqis during the Gulf War. Many soldiers were killed and several thousand others were taken as war prisoners. Those taken prisoner were released after the war ended. Other human dimensions of the war included some foreigners who left the country because of the war, but were not allowed to return after it was over.

Environmental Impact

The international allied force announced on February 26, 1991, that the invading Iraqi forces had been defeated and Kuwait had been liberated. In defeat, however, the retreating Iraqi army set fire to over 700 Kuwaiti oil wells. These fires were said to consume about 5 percent of the world's daily oil consumption every day they burned. About two million tons of carbon dioxide were emitted daily by the inferno. Valuable petroleum resources were lost, land was destroyed, and the atmosphere was polluted. Several million gallons of crude oil also flowed into the Persian Gulf, where it caused severe damage to both human and marine life, as well as fouling beaches.

Several other environmental changes have occurred since the war. Water resources in Kuwait, for example, have always been a challenge. The country has no fresh surface water resources. All fresh water comes from groundwater sources, or, more recently, by the desalinization of seawater. As a result of the war and the fires that followed, some groundwater deposits became contaminated. And Kuwait's desalinization plants were seriously damaged, thereby drastically reducing the available water supply. Repair of these plants received the highest priority following the end of hostilities.

The land surface was adversely affected in several ways. The presence of so many people in a fragile ecosystem led to a major disturbance of the system. Military tanks rolled over the land, chewing into its frail desert surface; foot soldiers dug large trenches in many places. The sparse vegetation was disturbed or destroyed, exposing the surface to the ravages of wind and water, including flooding after periods of rainfall. Sand began to be freely blown across the surface, dunes began to march across the landscape, and much of the country's limited soil resources were eroded. Following the war, attempts to find and remove war damage—including thousands of buried land mines—also contributed to the disturbance of the fragile soil that had suffered severely. Military vehicles damaged about 361 square miles (936 square kilometers) of the sandy desert surface, and another 1,363 square miles (3,530 square kilometers) of desert pavement was also degraded. In all, it is believed that about 30 percent of Kuwait's land surface area was adversely affected by the Gulf War.

Perhaps the greatest damage, however, was that inflicted by the oil leaks from damaged wells. Several hundred oil "lakes" formed during this time. There is great concern that chemicals contained in the oil may seep into the ground and contaminate the groundwater system. Besides contaminating the groundwater, the oil destroyed much of the plant cover, hence, the wildlife habitat. Thousands of migratory birds perished when they mistook oil lakes for water, or became fouled by oil floating on the gulf. The shallow seafloor became covered with oil—including the beautiful coral reefs, which suffered severe damage.

Humans, too, suffered from the environmental side effects of the war. The burning oil affected the air quality of Kuwait and the region. The air seemed to turn black from the smoke of burning wells. Swirls of desert dust combined with the smoke to turn the atmosphere into a choking, foul-smelling, acrid mixture of smoke and dust. Those prone to respiratory problems were particularly affected.

This view of modern Kuwait City shows the Liberation Tower, which was built after the end of the Gulf War.

9

Leisure Time in Kuwait

Kuwait is an arid land with beautiful coastlines along the Persian Gulf. Despite its small size and desert conditions, the country offers some wonderful sights and things to do. There are plenty of places where young people gather to spend time with friends and have fun. Most of the "action" takes place in or around Kuwait City or other urban centers nearby.

All kinds of food can be found in and around Kuwait City. Some of the restaurants and fast food places include menus that are familiar to Americans. They include chains like Applebee's, Chili's, TGI Friday, Fuddrucker, Pizza Hut, Burger King, and McDonald's. One can also sample plenty of local flavors by eating at any of the many local restaurants.

One way to learn more about a foreign land is to get impressions from people who have either visited or lived there. The following comments, summarized, are from people who have been to Kuwait. One thing visitors first notice is that the workweek extends from Saturday through Wednesday. Thursday is a "weekend" holiday and in the Islamic faith, Friday is a holy day of prayer. In the shops, visitors are often surprised by how inexpensive many items are, and there is no sales tax. Kuwait's major roads are modern in every respect, and roadsides are free of litter. Shopping malls or centers, restaurants, and other services line most of the major thoroughfares. Although most people who have visited Kuwait recommend the country as a vacation destination, they are quick to point out that searing hot temperatures and choking dust storms can occur. It is suggested that the best time to visit Kuwait is during the winter months to avoid the extreme weather.

If one visits Kuwait in February, temperatures are relatively cool—between 60 and 80°F (21 to 27°C). It is advised to plan a visit during a time other than during Ramadan (the Muslim fasting period). As is true in most countries during religious holidays, things can be very quiet—and Ramadan lasts an entire month. During this holiday, there is very little activity during the day when eating and drinking (any beverage) are not allowed.

Planning a Trip to Kuwait?

There are some important things to consider before leaving on a trip to Kuwait. Travelers need a passport, of course, and a visa—which can be obtained from the Kuwait Embassy in Washington, D.C. (For visas and for information on other entry requirements, you can contact the embassy at 2940 Tilden Street, NW, Washington D.C. 20008; phone 202-966-0702.) U.S. citizens are encouraged to register at the U.S. Embassy upon entering the country. This registration can be done online. Any child traveling to or from Kuwait must be accompanied by proper documentation.

This is to simplify entry and departure from the country. Travel to areas considered dangerous, such as near the Kuwait-Iraq border, is strongly discouraged.

Most Kuwaitis are friendly, especially if efforts are made to understand some of their culture. For more information on tips about traveling to Kuwait, check with your travel agent or visit the Kuwait Consular Information Sheet on the Internet.

Salmiya offers a large shopping complex located just a few minutes drive from Kuwait City. Other shopping areas include the Salhiah Shopping Complex, an elegant shopping mall with many stores that sell brand name products. The complex is connected to the Meridian Hotel. Other shopping malls include the Muthana Shopping Complex, the Al Sharq Shopping Complex and Marina, the Sultan Center in Salmiyah, the Sultan Center in Shwaikh, and the Salem Al Mubarek Street.

Many of the small shops do not accept credit cards. Here, unlike in the large malls, you could haggle over the price of items. Bargaining over the price of items can be lots of fun if the art is mastered. It is best to learn this how to haggle from a Kuwaiti friend if possible. He or she can explain the expectations and "rules."

Kuwait has many beautiful beaches where swimming is safe. The following beaches are highly recommended because they are clean and well maintained: the Sea Front, which extends along Gulf Road; and Green Island, also along Gulf Road, is a great place for young people to walk or spend an evening—it has a theater, a viewing tower, two restaurants, and a children's castle. Some beaches, for example the Shaab Sea Club and Ras Al Ardh Sea Club, require memberships. Other places to visit in Kuwait include the National Museum in Kuwait City, the Tareq Rajabv, Sadu House, the Grande Mosque, Kuwait Towers, Seif Palace, Failaka Island, and Al-Ahmadi. A visitor should

A visitor to Kuwait will find some familiar things, including several U.S. fast-food restaurants.

also visit a boat building company, since Kuwait is noted for pearl diving and boat building.

Sports

The most popular sport in Kuwait is football, or soccer as it is called in the United States. This game is played on both the professional and recreational levels. The national team has won two Gulf Cup regional football championships (1996 and 1998). Other sports played by the young include basketball, fencing, track and field, and swimming. Water sports are very common for those who live near the coast (about 90 percent of the population lives within an hour's drive from the coast). Some of the water sports include jet skiing, water skiing, and fishing. Because Kuwaitis love water, many families own their own beach apartments along the coast.

Recreation and Social Life

Kuwait's cities are quite active during the day, but the real social "action" takes place during the evenings, especially on weekends (Thursday and Friday). Much of the nightlife activity takes place along the coastline, especially at Salmiya and along the Gulf Road. People come to these areas for relaxation and fun. The influence of Western culture and society can be seen in many of the restaurants and shopping complexes that line this route.

During the day, the shopping malls, such as the Souq Sharg or Fanar complex, are busy with people scurrying about just as they do in malls elsewhere—walking, looking, stopping for a cup of coffee at Starbucks, and even shopping. Malls and most other shops are open Saturday through Thursday, 9:00 A.M. to 1:00 P.M. and again from 4:30 P.M. to 9:00 P.M.

People of all ages also gather at *maqahas* (traditional coffee shops). Young people prefer to hang out around Internet cafés that provide Internet access at a rate of approximately 2 KD (about $7.00). Clients can surf the Web, read, send email, or just or socialize. Internet cafés are very popular as they allow people to get in touch with the latest news from any part of the world and also get the chance to chat with one another.

In February 2001, fireworks exploded over the Persian Gulf as Kuwait celebrated the 10th anniversary of the end of the Gulf War and Kuwait's liberation from Iraq.

10

Kuwait Looks Ahead

T his small desert country will continue to play a major role on the global stage for some time to come. Although its area is small, it is rich in petroleum resources. As long as much of the world depends upon gas and oil to fuel its transportation and economy, Kuwait will benefit from its huge deposits of "black gold."

Despite Kuwait's hot, dry climate, its people have adapted well to the conditions. Most public places and homes are air-conditioned. Although it is expensive to produce, ample supplies of fresh water are available from desalinized seawater, of which there is an unlimited supply. Because of its prosperous oil-based economy, most Kuwaitis enjoy the same amenities as do most Americans.

The relationship between Kuwait and the United States should continue to be cordial. The two countries have many close economic ties. And most educated Kuwaitis are able to speak English, a fact that contributes to good communications between them and Americans.

Further, Kuwaitis realize that without American military intervention in 1990, the country might have fallen to Iraq. The younger generation, in particular, increasingly identifies with the Western world. Western media and the Internet are the two vehicles most responsible for this trend. Both serve to bring the country's youth in contact with the rest of the world. The tragic terrorist events that struck the United States on September 11, 2001, brought an outpouring of sympathy and outrage from the Kuwaitis. This suggests that links of friendship and respect continue to bind these two peoples. Despite its acceptance of some Western influences, Kuwait continues to be very much an Arabic nation. Islam and other Arab customs still exert their strong influence on the day-to-day life of Kuwaitis.

Kuwait is important regionally because of its strategic geographical location at the head of the Persian Gulf. With the Gulf War but a distant memory, and with stable oil prices, the country will continue to be a major world player in energy supply. For this reason, alone, it is important that the United States and Kuwait keep close ties. The United States needs the oil, and Kuwait depends on the United States and other Western countries for security in this troubled and often turbulent region of the world.

In looking ahead, perhaps the country's most urgent need is to diversify its economy. It must attract "clean" industries, such as those involving communications, finance, and other services. Tourism also holds much potential for economic growth. This small desert country can draw on its natural, historical, and cultural resources to attract visitors.

Facts at a Glance

Land and People

Full Country Name	The State of Kuwait
Area	6,880 sq mi (17,818 sq km)
Highest Point	1,000 feet (305 meters)
Population	2,041,961 (includes 1,159,913 non-national)
People	Kuwaiti (45%), other Arab (35%), Asian (9%)
Urban Population	98%
Life Expectancy	77 years
Capital	Kuwait City (population 238,000)
Major Cities	Kuwait City, Ras Al-Ardh, Al-Funaitis, Al-Fintas, Al-Khiran, Kadhmah, Al-Maqwa, Al-Ahmadi, and Al-Wafrah
Official Language	Arabic
Other Language	English
Religions	Muslim (85%), Christian, Hindu

Economy

Major Products	Petroleum
Gross Domestic Product	$32 billion
Economic Sectors	Petroleum, petrochemicals, desalinization
Currency	Kuwait dinar
Average Annual Income	Equal to U.S.$22,000

Government

Form of Government	Constitutional monarchy with a National Assembly serving as the legislative body
Head of State	Emir, Sheik Jaber al-Ahmad al-Jaber al-Sabah
Head of Government	Prime Minister, Crown Prince Saad al-Abdullah al-Salim al-Sabah
Voting Rights	All male citizens over age 18
Political Divisions	Administrative districts

325 B.C.E.*	Greeks lived on Failaka Island for the next two centuries.
250 B.C.E.	Persian Gulf was ruled by the Parthians, a powerful Persian dynasty.
632 A.D.	Muslim Arabs defeat the Persians.
1672	Kuwait City is established.
1752	Sabah bin Jaber from the Al-Sabah family is named the first ruler of Kuwait.
1899	Ottoman Empire tries to take control of Kuwait. Sheik Mubarak I requests protection from the British.
1913	Borders between Kuwait and Iraq are drawn up.
1914	Kuwait becomes a British protectorate following the outbreak of World War I.
1936	Drilling for oil started by the Anglo-Persian Oil Company of Great Britain and Gulf Oil (U.S.)
1946	First Kuwaiti commercial crude oil shipment was exported.
1961	Kuwait gains complete independence from Great Britain.
1962	First constitution of Kuwait is ratified.
1963	Kuwait joins the United Nations.
1966	Kuwait University is established.
1981	The Gulf Cooperation Council is formed with Kuwait and other Persian Gulf states.
1987	Military help from the United States is needed to protect Kuwait from attacks by Iran.
1990	*August 2:* Iraq invades Kuwait, beginning the Persian Gulf War.
1991	*January 17:* Allied forces begin "Operation Desert Storm" to liberate Kuwait.
	February 26: Kuwait is liberated

* Before the Common Era

Bibliography

CIA World Factbook. Kuwait 2000.

Foster, Leila Merrell. *Kuwait.* Enchantment of the World Second Series. Children's Press, 1998.

Hawley, T.A. *Against the Fires of Hell: The Environmental Disaster of the Gulf War.* Harcourt Brace Jovanovich, 1992.

Al-Mughani, Haya. *Women in Kuwait. The Politics of Gender.* London: Saqi Books, 1993.

O'Shea, Maria. *Kuwait.* Cultures of the World, 1999.

Powell, Colin. *My American Journey.* Random House, 1995.

Websites

http://lcweb2.loc.gov/frd/cs/kwtoc/html
(Library of Congress)

http://www.kuwaitdaily.com/
(Daily news about Kuwait)

http://www.usembassy.gov.kw
(Travel information from the U.S. Embassy)

The following sites provide general information about Kuwait.

http://www.cia.gov/cia/publications/factbook/geos/ku.html

http://www.eia.doe.gov/emen/cabs/kuwait.html

http://www.kuwaitonline.com

http://www.arab.net/kuwait/Kuwait_contents.html

http://encarta.msn.com

Index

Picture Credits

SOLOMON A. ISIORHO teaches Geography and Geology courses at Indiana University-Purdue University, Fort Wayne (IPFW) and is currently an associate professor of Geosciences. He has a strong interest in writing children books in the sciences and loves to travel. His travels have taken him to four continents so far from the tropics to arid regions of the world.

CHARLES F. "FRITZ" GRITZNER is Distinguished Professor of Geography at South Dakota State University. He is now in his fifth decade of college teaching and research. Much of his career work has focused on geographic education. Fritz has served as both president and executive director of the National Council for Geographic Education and has received the Council's George J. Miller Award for Distinguished Service..